Praise for *Introducing Mindfulness: Buddhist Background and Practical Exercises*

Introducing Mindfulness is an important read for anyone looking to further their conceptual understanding, link it with practice, and in doing so deepen their wisdom. Seamlessly weaving together primary texts, memorable stories and practical practice tips ranging from eating to ethics, Anālayo brings a fresh pragmatism to a field easily waylaid by dogmatism. – **Judson Brewer**, author of *The Craving Mind*

Although we often speak of "mindfulness" in the singular, it manifests in a variety of ways in contexts ranging from the simple act of eating a meal to the contemplation of the mind itself. Meticulously researched and written with striking lucidity, this book by a renowned scholar-practitioner guides us through the intricacies of mindfulness with explanations and exercises that, while remarkably accessible to those who are new to mindfulness, are at the same filled with keen insights relevant to even the most accomplished practitioners and researchers. Bhikkhu Anālayo examines fundamental questions, such as the way that key capacities of mindfulness can emerge from working with our reactivity to pain, and he does so by also tracing pivotal historical developments that explain how various traditions interpret mindfulness. Always returning to the concrete goal of actually cultivating mindfulness, this remarkable book dispels many misunderstandings – such as the notion that it is somehow "inauthentic" to practice mindfulness for health reasons – while offering a clear, practical and insightful account of how we can ourselves be more mindful. – **John D Dunne**, Distinguished Professor of Contemplative Humanities, University of Wisconsin–Madison

In *Introducing Mindfulness*, Anālayo offers a wide-ranging survey of both the meaning and applications of mindfulness. It is a wise and helpful presentation of essential elements of the Buddha's teaching, and it will be of great value for those who wish to put these teachings into practice. A wonderful Dharma gift. – **Joseph Goldstein**, author of *Mindfulness: A Practical Guide to Awakening*

This monograph is a gold mine for anyone who is working in the broad field of mindfulness-based programs for addressing health and wellbeing in the face of suffering – in any or all of its guises. It is a concise yet comprehensive high-resolution exegesis of the major pillars of classical dharma through the lens of mindfulness, offered by a highly respected scholar/practitioner monastic. It is an invaluable primer and reference text for anyone interested in the breadth and depth of mindfulness itself, its original Buddhist sources, its ethical foundation, its universal applicability, and its incontestable relevance in our world today. – **Jon Kabat-Zinn**, author of *Meditation Is Not What You Think: Mindfulness and Why It Is So Important*, and *Falling Awake: How to Practice Mindfulness in Everyday Life*

This is a timely book for understanding the Buddhist background of mindfulness and how to integrate its practice into our daily lives. Venerable Anālayo provides an extraordinarily clear and readable guide to mindfulness in accessible language that is informed by his scholarship in early Buddhism and grounded in his extensive personal meditation practice. For those who want to deepen their understanding of mindfulness, this book is a rare treat. It may well be the best scholarly yet practical introduction to the topic. – **Nirbhay N. Singh**, Editor-in-Chief of the journal *Mindfulness*

INTRODUCING MINDFULNESS:

Also by Bhikkhu Anālayo:

Satipaṭṭhāna, The Direct Path to Realization
The Genesis of the Bodhisattva Ideal
A Comparative Study of the Majjhima-nikāya
Excursions into the Thought-world of the Pāli Discourses
Madhyama-āgama Studies
Perspectives on Satipaṭṭhāna
The Dawn of Abhidharma
Compassion and Emptiness in Early Buddhist Meditation
Saṃyukta-āgama Studies
Ekottarika-āgama Studies
The Foundation History of the Nuns' Order
Mindfully Facing Disease and Death
Buddhapada and the Bodhisattva Path
Early Buddhist Meditation Studies
Dīrgha-āgama Studies
Vinaya Studies
A Meditator's Life of the Buddha
Rebirth in Early Buddhism and Current Research
Satipaṭṭhāna Meditation: A Practice Guide
Bhikkhunī Ordination from Ancient India to Contemporary Sri Lanka
Mindfulness of Breathing: A Practice Guide and Translations
Mindfully Facing Climate Change
Mindfulness in Early Buddhism: Characteristics and Functions

Bhikkhu Analayo

INTRODUCING MINDFULNESS:

Buddhist Background and Practical Exercises

Ⓦ

Windhorse Publications
info@windhorsepublications.com
windhorsepublications.com

As an act of Dhammadāna, Anālayo has waived royalty
payments for this book.

The index was not compiled by the author.

Drawings by Dido Dolmen
(www.didodolmen.it)
Cover design by Dhammarati

Typesetting and layout by Tarajyoti
Printed by Bell & Bain Ltd, Glasgow

British Library Cataloguing in Publication Data:
A catalogue record for this book is available from
the British Library.

ISBN: 978-1-911407-57-7

CONTENTS

ABOUT THE AUTHOR

Born in 1962 in Germany, Bhikkhu Anālayo was ordained in 1995 in Sri Lanka, and completed a PhD on the *Satipaṭṭhāna-sutta* at the University of Peradeniya, Sri Lanka, in 2000 – published in 2003 by Windhorse Publications under the title *Satipaṭṭhāna, The Direct Path to Realization*.

Anālayo is a professor of Buddhist Studies; his main research area is early Buddhism and in particular the topics of the Chinese *Āgama*s, meditation, and women in Buddhism. Besides his academic pursuits, he regularly teaches meditation. He presently resides at the Barre Center for Buddhist Studies in Massachusetts, where he spends most of his time in silent retreat.

ACKNOWLEDGEMENT

I am indebted to Chris Burke, Bhikkhunī Dhammadinnā, Ann Dillon, Joseph Goldstein, Linda Grace, Jon Kabat-Zinn, and Yuka Nakamura for commenting on a draft version of this book and to the staff, board members, and supporters of the Barre Center for Buddhist Studies for providing me with the facilities needed to do my practice and writing.

PUBLISHER'S ACKNOWLEDGEMENTS

Windhorse Publications wishes to gratefully acknowledge a grant from the Triratna European Chairs' Assembly Fund and the Future Dharma Fund towards the production of this book.

We also wish to acknowledge and thank the individual donors who gave to the book's production via our "Sponsor-a-book" campaign.

FOREWORD BY JACK KORNFIELD

For all who are interested in the Buddhist roots of mindfulness practice, this is an important book and a welcome gift. As mindfulness has spread in the West, it is most frequently portrayed as an eyes closed interior meditation practice, used primarily for bringing calm or reducing stress. When other uses of mindfulness are taught they are often considered to be modern creations or unorthodox approaches, and not the real thing.

Fortunately for us, as Bhikkhu Anālayo illuminates in this book, the very fabric of mindfulness and of a mindfulness life, as laid out in the comprehensive teachings of the Buddha, is much broader than this. It includes mindfulness of diet and bodily movement, mindfulness in relation to healing, mindful approaches to compassionate relationship and community. It includes mindful livelihood, mindful reflection, and mindful awareness of the workings of mind and the nature of consciousness itself.

There are remarkable gifts found in this book as in all of Bhikkhu Anālayo's writing. He is a deep practitioner and a world-renowned scholar who is able to read and compare the earliest Buddhist teachings in several ancient languages, and can bring a richness of understanding to these foundational texts. And more remarkably for a scholar, he doesn't cling to fixed positions but shows us, so we can see for ourselves, the many useful perspectives found across these early texts.

This approach is in keeping with the multiple ways the Buddha himself offered teachings. In different circumstances over forty-five years, the Buddha varied his skillful means widely, always responding to the needs of those he taught. In certain situations of human difficulty, he would encourage engaged loving care for one another, and then in other difficult situations he would counsel removing yourself from attachment. Sometimes he encouraged his students to make fierce effort like their hair was on fire, and at other times he directed students to practice with ease and tender letting go. Sometimes he focused on mindfulness of decay and death, sometimes on mindfully cultivating joy.

Mindfulness was at the center of what he taught. As a consummate teacher, psychologist, healer, and guide to liberation, the Buddha offered many different forms of mindfulness training. Bhikkhu Anālayo shows us how broadly it was taught as a universal medicine for understanding, applicable in multiple dimensions, foremost as the gateway to liberation.

There are parallels to this early breadth of mindfulness now apparent as mindfulness training has spread across the modern world. As a Buddhist teacher and Western psychologist, I have delighted in seeing how Buddhist mindfulness and Dharma principles are being incorporated into psychological clinical work, in cognitive therapy, in traditions of physical and emotional healing, self compassion and deep healing presence, in fostering the whole field of positive psychology. Programs like Mindfulness-Based Eating Awareness Training (MB-EAT) used for eating disorders, and Mindfulness-Based Cognitive Therapy (MBCT) used for depression, are obvious examples. In the same way, the transformative power of mindfulness training has spread to offer benefits in the realms of medicine, in business and in education, in the arts and in the creation of healthy community. The seeds for this widespread use of mindfulness are all found in the early teachings, and the benefits were understood to be universal.

Bhikkhu Anālayo also shows how the breadth of mindfulness evolved in the blossoming of the Mahāyāna traditions. Mahāyāna's growing emphasis on the bodhisattva ideal, the increasing focus on compassion, and the later non-dual traditions of practice all have sources and antecedents in the early texts and the multiple skillful teachings of mindfulness.

A special dimension of this manuscript are the practices and exercises offered at the conclusion of each chapter. This is the most important point. These ancient and now modern liberating teachings are not to be simply read. They are to be practiced.

Bhikkhu Analayo offers simple skilled mindfulness practices for each of the dimensions of this book. Open-minded practices of embodied mindfulness are described, beginning with eating and health, and continuing with mindfulness examining mind and body, our relation to death, and the nature of the mind itself. Significantly, by highlighting the earliest teachings on internal and external mindfulness, Bhikkhu Anālayo shows how, individually and collectively, we can use mindfulness to bring a liberating understanding to ourselves and to the pressing problems of our global, social, modern world. We need this more than ever.

Read these essays slowly.
Enjoy their wisdom, intelligence and inspiration.
Reflect on them and put them into practice.

In this you will find many blessings
to which I add my own.

With *mettā*,
Jack Kornfield
Spirit Rock Center, 2019

INTRODUCTION

The aim of this book is to provide information on the early Buddhist background to mindfulness, together with practical exercises, for those who have benefitted from doing a programme in mindfulness or are involved in teaching or research related to such programmes. I have endeavoured to make my presentation of chief aspects of mindfulness accessible to those who may have only a basic familiarity with Buddhist teachings and are not necessarily acquainted with all the relevant specific notions and terminology. Whenever specific Buddhist terms or ideas come up in the course of my discussion, I try my best to explain them. Inline references to my other publications are meant to enable readers to follow up a topic of particular interest for further study.

My presentation is based on sources that reflect "early Buddhism", which stands for roughly the first two centuries in the history of Buddhism, from about the fifth to the third century before the common era. The main historical evidence for these first two centuries are the "early discourses", together with the relatively few artefacts and archaeological remains of Buddhist sites that are also from the same period or shortly thereafter. The early discourses go back to instructions and teachings given orally by the Buddha and his disciples. In those times in India, writing was not in use for such purposes, and so over the centuries these teachings were transmitted orally. The final results of such oral transmission are available to us nowadays in the form of written texts, probably the best-known collection of which are the "Pāli discourses", Pāli being an ancient Indian language.

These orally transmitted early discourses provide a range of perspectives on mindfulness. A clear overarching concern in them is the role of mindfulness in the path to "awakening", in the sense of awakening to an understanding of reality as it is. Another term for the goal of the Buddhist path of practice is "liberation", which conveys the sense of freedom of the mind from the bondage of what are considered three root defilements: greed, anger, and delusion. According to the early Buddhist analysis, being under the influence of these defilements leads to acting in ways that are detrimental for ourselves and others. Mindfulness is a central tool to recognize such influence and emerge from it, by way of bringing about a clear vision of reality and fostering a gradual freeing of the mind from bondage.

Early Buddhist doctrine conceives the path to liberation from these defilements as an eightfold one, in the sense that the systematic cultivation of mindfulness takes place in collaboration with another seven factors of the path. In other words, mindfulness operates in concert with other qualities and practices, a considerable number of which concern ethical behaviour. As the seventh factor of this path, mindfulness takes the form of four "establishments of mindfulness" (*satipaṭṭhāna*). These direct mindful contemplation to the body (1), to feeling tones in the sense of the affective dimension of experience (2), to states of mind (3), and to "dharmas" (4). The last relates to specific Buddhist teachings, called collectively the "Dharma", on how to orient the mind towards liberation.

The eightfold path to liberation comes embedded in another teaching. This is known as the "four noble truths", which according to tradition was the first teaching given by the Buddha after his awakening. The notion of four truths appears to have been modelled on an ancient Indian medical diagnostic scheme.

Underlying this diagnostic scheme is the principle of causality or "dependent arising". Early Buddhist thought holds that all we do and experience is the product of causes and conditions. Some of these conditions are amenable to our intentional influence, and it is here that mindfulness can have a substantial impact.

In subsequent chapters I will come back in more detail to these aspects of early Buddhist doctrine. The above brief survey is just meant to provide a first sketch of the most relevant teachings.

The path to liberation as the main concern of the early Buddhist teachings is not the only setting in which mindfulness can unfold its beneficial potential. It can also be employed for such common medical purposes as weight reduction through mindful eating, which was already a recognized dimension of mindfulness in early Buddhist thought. As this provides a precedent for the current clinical uses of mindfulness, I begin with this topic in the first chapter in this book. In Chapters 2 and 3 I turn to the ethics of mindfulness and the relationship between mindfulness and compassion.

Based on the groundwork laid in these first three chapters, in Chapters 4 to 6 I examine the three themes of embodied mindfulness, the relationship between mindfulness and focused attention (as evident in instructions for mindfulness of breathing), and the connection between mindfulness and wisdom (underlying the practice of the four establishments of mindfulness). These three topics are meant to lead to a gradually deepening appreciation of early Buddhist dimensions of formal mindfulness practice.

Chapters 7 to 9 are dedicated to more specific aspects of mindfulness. These are the significance of bare awareness (I use "awareness" here and elsewhere as a synonym for "mindfulness"), the relationship between mindfulness and health, and the cultivation of mindfulness of death. Each of these brings out particular dimensions of the early Buddhist use of mindfulness that remain relevant today.

In the final three chapters I try to sketch a basic history of mindfulness. Chapter 10 begins with pre-Buddhist precedents and then relates the Buddha's quest for awakening to mindfulness. Chapter 11 proceeds from the time of the Buddha to modern-day insight meditation practices (also known by the Pāli term *vipassanā*), which spread from South and Southeast Asia to the West. Here I try to outline the doctrinal developments that appear to have led to the particular form of mindfulness cultivated in these insight meditation traditions. Chapter 12 then pursues the historical development from early Buddhism to non-dual practices in Himalayan and East Asian Buddhist traditions, known under such names as the "Great Perfection" or else as "Zen" (with its predecessors in "Chán" and "Son"). These three chapters are meant to show the variety of mindfulness models in the Buddhist traditions, all of which have as their starting point the rich and multifaceted early Buddhist teachings on mindfulness.

Mindfulness is something that requires practice in order to be understood. For this reason, at the end of each chapter of my exploration I present practice instructions. The sequence of the chapters in this book aligns with the gradual evolution of these instructions, so that a step-by-step development of mindfulness results. These instructions serve to deepen a practical understanding of the key aspects of mindfulness and make these a matter of personal experience.

The progression of practice instructions falls into four groups of three. The first triad (Chapters 1 to 3) relates to daily-life mindfulness practices, in the sense that these can be implemented easily as they do not require setting aside time for formal meditation. The second triad (Chapters 4 to 6) introduces whole-body awareness and mindfulness of breathing as somewhat more formal meditation practices. Instructions given in subsequent chapters continue to relate to being mindful of the breath in various ways. The third triad (Chapters 7 to 9) combines the experience of the breath with specific applications of mindfulness. The final triad (Chapters 10 to 12) contains instructions for exploring different approaches to mindfulness that evolved in the course of history from their common early Buddhist ancestor.

In the conclusion I bring the different strands of my exploration together and relate these to the contemporary spread of mindfulness as well as to the current situation we as human beings are confronted with on this planet. I believe mindfulness has much to offer to enable us to face the current ecological and climatic crisis.

I

MINDFUL EATING

In this first chapter, I begin my exploration of mindfulness in early Buddhist thought with a discourse that reports how the Buddha taught mindfulness to an overeating lay disciple, a king by the name of Pasenadi. The teaching given by the Buddha, and its successful implementation by the king, is significant beyond the actual issue of overeating, as it puts into perspective the contemporary use of mindfulness for health purposes. Such employment has at times met with some degree of scepticism in traditional Buddhist circles and even given rise to apprehensions of being a misappropriation of a religious practice that was never intended for secular purposes. The story of King Pasenadi helps to put such apprehensions to rest.

After surveying the story of King Pasenadi, I examine the actual instructions given on this occasion. Then I turn to the benefits of mindful eating in general and mindful tasting in particular. The different dimensions of mindfulness that emerge during these explorations lead me to the relationship between mindfulness and memory. By way of rounding off my discussion in this chapter, I take up a central Buddhist teaching reflecting an ancient Indian medical diagnostic scheme. This teaching is known as the "four noble truths", which I relate to the practice of mindful eating.

KING PASENADI OVEREATS

The early discourses report that a disciple of the Buddha and local king by the name of Pasenadi was partaking of an excessive amount of food (see Anālayo 2018b, 2018e, 2019e, and 2020d: 175–181). On one occasion, after having indulged in overeating, he went to visit the Buddha. Due to having eaten way too much, he was panting. The Buddha noticed his condition and responded by delivering a verse on the need for continuous mindfulness to know measure with food, which in turn will improve his longevity.

King Pasenadi asked another young man, present on this occasion, to memorize the verse and recite it every time food was being served, promising a regular payment for this service. The young man did as he was told. On being repeatedly reminded of the need for mindfulness when eating, King Pasenadi learned to reduce the amount of food he was taking and became slimmer. The discourse concludes with King Pasenadi stroking his body and expressing his gratitude for the benefit he had gained from the Buddha's instruction.

This episode clearly shows that in the ancient Indian setting instructions on mindfulness were already aimed at mundane health issues. Expressed in contemporary terminology, the

Buddha is on record for devising a mindfulness-based practice to reduce overeating, and this successfully achieves weight reduction. In addition, the narrative involves another person who takes on a role comparable to a mindfulness trainer. He even receives regular payment for repeating, in the presence of the king, the instructions on mindfulness given by the Buddha. The different elements in this episode provide a precedent for the contemporary employment of mindfulness for achieving health benefits.

INSTRUCTIONS ON MINDFUL EATING

According to the relevant Pāli discourse, the actual instruction given by the Buddha on this occasion is as follows (Anālayo 2018b: 39):

> People who are constantly mindful
> Know their measure with the food they have gotten.
> Their feeling tones become attenuated;
> They age slowly and guard their longevity.

The reference to "feeling tones" here does not intend emotions. Instead, it stands for the affective tone of what is experienced. This tone can be either pleasant, or unpleasant, or else neither of the two: neutral. In the present context, the relevant feeling tones are in particular unpleasant ones. These could be resulting from hunger or from overeating. By knowing our measure with food, such feeling tones can become attenuated. The pangs of hunger will no longer be felt, nor will the unpleasant feeling tones that result from eating too much.

In order to achieve this aim, the verse instruction points to the need to be mindful, in fact to be "constantly" mindful. It is precisely through establishing continuity in mindfulness that it becomes possible to recognize clearly at what point we have had enough. Overeating more easily occurs when being absentminded. The antidote is countering such absentmindedness by cultivating mental presence through mindfulness.

BENEFITS OF MINDFUL EATING

A central function of mindfulness here is to accompany the process of eating with mental presence and awareness. Such presence of mindfulness helps to discern clearly the taste of the food and the signals given by the body when being nourished. As sensations of hunger gradually abate, sooner or later the body will give signs of becoming full. If these are noticed with mindfulness, it becomes evident when the right amount has been eaten. It also becomes a matter of direct personal experience that going beyond that amount creates discomfort. Eating in this way shows the ability of mindfulness to bring us fully in touch with what is taking place. This happens simply through establishing mental presence, instead of switching off mentally and acting absentmindedly.

Continuous presence of mindfulness will also ensure that food is chewed properly, instead of gulped down quickly and the next spoonful immediately reached for, even before the present one has been properly chewed. Here mindfulness helps us to slow down. Slowing down is another of the characteristic functions of mindfulness that is particularly helpful in forestalling hasty reactions and countering the acting out of detrimental habits. In relation to food, this need not be taken to the extremes of slow-motion eating, but can simply become a way of reducing haste, leading to a deliberate and unhurried way of taking meals. With mindfulness established, it becomes more and more natural to chew properly before swallowing, so as to make sure the food is well prepared for proper digestion.

Besides serving to attenuate unpleasant feeling tones, the instructions also connect such mindfulness practice with the benefits of ageing slowly and having a long life. These longer-term benefits go beyond the immediate discomfort caused by overeating. They throw into relief the importance given in this instruction to mundane health benefits as the outcome of mindfulness practice. In this way, the cultivation of mindfulness can have both immediate and long-term benefits.

MINDFUL TASTING

Another aspect of applying mindfulness to a simple daily activity like eating relates to the experience of tasting the food eaten. The curriculum of Mindfulness-Based Stress Reduction includes an exercise that shows this potential. The exercise requires slowly and attentively chewing a raisin. Kabat-Zinn (1990/2013: 15) reports that this simple exercise made people realize the following:

> They actually experienced what a raisin tasted like for the first time that they could remember … often someone makes the connection that if we ate like that all the time, we would eat less and have more pleasant and satisfying experiences of food.

From a medical viewpoint, tasting is an integral aspect of the preparatory phase of proper digestion, when the food is still in the mouth, as it leads to an increase in gastric secretion. By establishing mindfulness when eating, this process can be allowed to fulfil its function properly. In this way, mindfulness can help to restore a healthy relationship to eating and at the same time improve physical health.

Here it is also of interest how the Buddha himself related to the taste of food (Anālayo 2017g: 202). He fully experienced the taste, yet without having any craving for the taste. The example set by the Buddha in this way can serve as an inspiration for cultivating mindful eating.

Such mindful eating can reveal an important dimension of mindfulness, namely of being rooted in the present moment. Instead of mentally wandering off into past or future experiences and related associations, with mindfulness established while eating it becomes possible to be fully with the present moment's taste. Since this taste is happening right now, just being with it automatically takes us right into the midst of the here and now. In spite of its simplicity, mindful tasting can become a powerful tool for grounding ourselves every time we take our daily meals.

Because of having been fully with this moment's taste when eating, it also becomes easier to let go of the taste once it has come to its natural termination. Having been cultivated while eating, the ability to remain fully in the here and now through mindfulness can then be allowed to spread to a range of other activities. The cultivation of being with mindfulness in the present moment has manifold repercussions and is of central importance to its meditative practice in the form of the four establishments of mindfulness (Anālayo 2019d), a topic I will explore in more detail in a subsequent chapter.

MINDFULNESS AND MEMORY

The practice of mindful eating can bring out yet another significant dimension of mindfulness, which is its potential to strengthen memory (see Anālayo 2017c: 26–34, 2018c, 2018d, 2018h, and 2020d: 11–46). Mindfulness can have such an effect in two interrelated ways. One of these is that, due to establishing an attitude of open receptivity, mindfulness makes it easier for relevant information to come to mind. The other contribution to be made by mindfulness relates to what is to be recalled. The more mindful we are when something happens, the easier it will be to remember later what took place.

An illustrative example of this potential is the exercise of mindfully eating a raisin, mentioned above. Unlike thousands of raisins eaten absentmindedly on earlier occasions, the experience of mindfully tasting this one raisin can be such an extraordinary experience that it will be remembered even after a long time. What made this experience stand out was not the raisin itself, which of course was not substantially different from other raisins, but the presence of mindfulness. Such mindful eating led some participants in this exercise to the realization that they had never really tasted a raisin before. The increased intake of information that results from deliberate paying attention highlights this potential of mindfulness to strengthen memory.

The relationship to memory that emerges in this way reveals an important facet of mindfulness. Being mindful means to act with such attentiveness that later we are able to remember clearly. Suppose we are listening to a talk and are expected to summarize it later (without relying on recording equipment). Given such a task, we would try our best to stay present and not get sidetracked. Suppose again that we are walking a path for the first time with the help of a guide, knowing that the next time we will have to find the way alone. In such a situation it is vital to notice clearly and then remember which turns to take. This is precisely what can be accomplished through mindfulness, namely fully taking in the available information in such a way that it can later easily be retrieved.

RIGHT VIEW

Although not explicitly mentioned in the discourse to King Pasenadi, the problem of overeating and the potential of mindfulness for addressing it could be captured with a teaching of central importance in Buddhist doctrine. This teaching is known under the name of "right view". The basic idea here is that, in order to act in ways that benefit, rather than harm, ourselves and others, we need to be able to *view* things from the *right* perspective.

When defining the parameters of such right perspective, the Buddha is on record for having employed a diagnostic scheme apparently in use in ancient Indian medicine. The basic features of this diagnostic scheme, which has similarities with a framework used in modern-day medicine, can be summarized as comprising the following four aspects: diagnosis, etiology, prognosis, and treatment plan.

The Buddha apparently adopted this ancient Indian scheme of diagnosis in what is recorded as being his very first teaching after having awakened, formulated as the "four noble truths" (Anālayo 2015c: 347–388, 2016a: 267–299, and 2016b: 9–16). Applied to the human predicament, the teaching on these four noble truths can be understood to involve recognition of the following:

1) diagnosis: the distressful repercussions of whatever difficulty we are facing,

2) etiology: how we are contributing to that distress through craving and attachment,

3) prognosis: the potential to reduce the distress by cultivating a different attitude,

4) treatment plan: the path of practice to be undertaken to achieve this aim.

In the case of eating, a first step to be taken is to recognize clearly the distress overeating causes us and its detrimental effects on our health. Whatever other conditions might trigger overeating, we can learn to take responsibility for our reactions to them. Taking responsibility in this way comes together with the clear recognition that it is in principle possible *not* to act on these impulses. A practice to achieve the not acting out of impulses is to establish mindfulness while eating, in line with the instructions given to King Pasenadi.

In this way, the teaching on the four noble truths can be meaningfully applied to overeating as well as other situations. The basic principle is to recognize clearly and honestly the actual manifestation of distress (1). Next, we identify how we ourselves contribute to that. What are the causes and conditions leading to the distress and which of these can be changed (2)? This in turn leads to a vision of our goal: emerging from the experience of distress (3). Proceeding towards that goal then requires that we take practical steps that enable us to reduce and eventually overcome those detrimental habit patterns that tend to cause our distress (4).

SUMMARY

Relating mindfulness to mundane activities like eating, with an aim to benefit health, is already an early Buddhist practice and not a recent innovation. Undertaking such practice reveals several key aspects of mindfulness. One of these is the potential of mindfulness to get us in touch with what is happening by establishing mental clarity, rather than switching off mentally and going into autopilot mode. A related aspect is that mindfulness can help us remain rooted in the present moment instead of wandering off into the past or the future. Moreover, it can introduce an element of slowing down and thereby help us to come to our senses. With mindfulness established, we learn to be receptive in such a way that it becomes easier to remember later what happened.

PRACTICE SUGGESTIONS

The times when we take our meals can be convenient opportunities for gradually introducing mindfulness in our lives, if we are able to eat without having to rush to finish our meal as soon as possible. To begin with, it would be ideal to eat in silence, although eventually it will be possible to be mindful at least intermittently when eating in the company of others who are engaged in conversations. Using mealtimes to develop mindfulness enables us to introduce this quality into our life without needing to set aside special times or to find an appropriate place or particular posture. After having experienced for ourselves the benefits of mindfulness, we will then more easily be motivated to set aside time and space for its further cultivation. To get started, however, it seems best to begin in a low-key manner, by simply making mindfulness our companion when we are sitting down to eat anyway.

With mindfulness established on such occasions, we gradually begin to explore the different aspects of eating. How is the food apperceived before being taken into the mouth? How does it taste when placed in the mouth? Can it be properly chewed before we reach out for the next spoonful? This exploration can take the form of a gradual unfolding, comparable to the petals of a flower in the sun. It need not be at all stressful or demanding. All that is required is to shine the rays of mindfulness on the present moment to the extent to which this is possible. There are days when we are too tired or too stressed to explore this fully. We need not feel any negativity; we simply recognize that this is the present situation. But after days of cloudy weather and rain, sooner or later the sun will emerge again. Similarly, sooner or later it will become possible again to partake of the enriching presence of mindfulness during our meal.

Frequently practising in this way, we can see for ourselves the benefits of mindfulness. We can experience more fully the taste of the meal without undue craving for the taste. Our bodily health improves, as we come to recognize when we have had enough. In this way food can fulfil its proper function, which is to sustain the body. From having been established with regard to eating, slowly mindfulness can be allowed to extend its beneficial effects to other domains of our lives. To some of these I turn in the next chapter.

II

THE ETHICS OF MINDFULNESS

In the last chapter, an exploration of mindfulness in relation to eating led me to a brief look at a central teaching of early Buddhism, which is "right view" in the form of the "four noble truths". In what follows I pursue in particular the fourth of these truths, concerning the actual path of practice. This puts into context the cultivation of mindfulness which, in early Buddhist thought, is strongly embedded in morality or ethics.

I begin by again taking up the case of King Pasenadi, placing the instruction given to him on mindful eating in relation to what other discourses indicate about his personality and the type of teachings he received on other occasions from the Buddha. Then I examine the need for an ethical foundation for mindfulness when it is being cultivated as part of the early Buddhist path to liberation. I also explore the practical implications of directing mindfulness either internally or else externally. From the role of ethics as a foundation for mindfulness practice, I then turn to a complementary perspective, where moral conduct itself becomes an object of mindful recollection.

TEACHINGS TO KING PASENADI

The early discourses report a series of encounters between the Buddha and King Pasenadi, making it possible to put the instruction on mindfulness of eating, given to him, in a broader context (see Anālayo 2020d: 180f). A survey of the various encounters between these two, as reported in the discourses, conveys the impression that mindful eating might be the only actual meditation teaching the king received, at least in so far as such teachings are recorded at all. Exchanges during other encounters with the Buddha touch on a variety of themes but tend to have little to do with meditation.

Moreover, the impression conveyed by the relevant discourses is that Pasenadi still pursued the typical activities of a petty king in ancient India, including warfare. Fighting a war is not easily reconciled with the basic moral conduct of a Buddhist lay disciple, which requires training oneself in five precepts. The first of these is abstaining from intentionally killing any living being (the remaining precepts concern not stealing, not engaging in sexual activity of the type that harms others, not speaking falsehood, and not taking intoxicants).

Another passage, not related to King Pasenadi, reports the Buddha taking an unequivocally strong stance against warfare, pointing to the harmful karmic consequence a warrior incurs when engaging in battle (Anālayo 2009a). This makes it fairly safe to assume that lay disciples fully committed to putting into practice the Buddha's teaching would be well advised to refrain from warfare. Yet, even though he must have been aware of Pasenadi's military activities, the Buddha apparently had no qualms about teaching mindful eating to the king.

BUILDING AN ETHICAL FOUNDATION

This certainly does not mean that building an ethical foundation is not of central importance in early Buddhist practice and an essential requirement for the cultivation of mindfulness as part of the path to liberation (which in early Buddhist thought stands for complete and irreversible freedom of the mind from defiled mental conditions). Several discourses report the Buddha demanding of his monastic disciples that they ensure being well grounded in morality as a basis for intensive meditation practice. One discourse even goes so far as to state that the whole purpose of the Buddha's teachings on morality is to support the formal cultivation of mindfulness (see Anālayo 2018i: 148 and 2020d: 133f). Such formal cultivation involves four "establishments of mindfulness", which are contemplation of the body, feeling tones, states of mind, and dharmas (specific Buddhist teachings); I will explore these in more detail in a subsequent chapter. A baseline condition for their cultivation is that maintaining moral conduct results in freedom from regret, which supports meditative practice in general.

The case of King Pasenadi shows that receiving instructions on mindfulness for mundane purposes like health improvement was not made dependent on first having established a firm foundation in ethical restraint. This suggests that the role played by ethics in relation to mindfulness practice aligns with the purposes such practice is meant to serve. If it is just a measure of health improvement, then it does not seem to be mandatory to adopt the same high ethical standards required for those who have embarked on the path to liberation. This certainly does not mean that ethical restraint can simply be dismissed as irrelevant. In fact ethical conduct and mindfulness practice are closely interrelated. Genuinely cultivating mindfulness will naturally increase sensitivity to ethical concerns and improve one's ability and willingness to strengthen one's moral conduct. In short, it is all a matter of gradual growth.

Here it is also relevant to note that the question at stake concerns not just the difference between ethical trainings for lay disciples and for monastics. One discourse reports a lay disciple who was a proficient practitioner of the four establishments of mindfulness, having reached a level of mental purity that made it impossible to kill even an insect intentionally (Anālayo 2016b: 70). Such a person would have been incapable of doing battle or engaging in some of the sensual activities in which King Pasenadi still indulged.

The high level of attainment reached by this lay disciple is one of several instances showing that early Buddhist instructions on the four establishments of mindfulness were not solely aimed at monastics. Because such instructions tend to be addressed to monastics, the impression can easily arise that they are only meant for them. However, such modes of address need to be understood from the viewpoint of ancient Indian etiquette. When speaking to a crowd of people, this etiquette apparently required addressing those who were considered to be most worthy of respect in the assembly (Collett and Anālayo 2014). Such a custom can even take the form of addressing a group of friends by the name of their leader, whose name will then be put in the plural. In other words, when teachings on the four establishments of mindfulness are addressed to monastics, such instructions were also intended for lay practitioners.

INTERNAL AND EXTERNAL MINDFULNESS

Not only monastics, but also lay disciples need to fulfil higher standards of moral conduct if they take on full-time practice of mindfulness. In fact, ethics is an integral part of such dedicated practice. The ways we act and speak, how we interrelate with others, all of these need to become what I like to call "mindfulness-supportive behaviour". This in turn relates to the fourth of the four noble truths, mentioned in the last chapter. The fourth truth concerns the actual path of practice to be undertaken in order to achieve a gradual diminishing of craving and attachment.

 In early Buddhist thought, the practical demands of this fourth truth are explained in terms of a "noble eightfold path". This path leads to inner nobility of the mind; it is eightfold in so far as it comprises eight factors, as follows:

1) right view
2) right intention
3) right speech
4) right action
5) right livelihood
6) right effort
7) right mindfulness
8) right concentration

A basic understanding of the four noble truths is the first factor of this path: "right view". The second factor is "right intention", which reflects the importance of our volitions and choices. These need to be aligned with the basic diagnostic perspective afforded by the four noble truths. With the diagnostic perspective of right view informing our intentions and aims, the direction is well set for orienting our speech (3), action (4), and livelihood (5) accordingly. These three factors of the noble eightfold path are especially relevant to ethical behaviour.

The need to streamline words, deeds, and ways of earning an income in such a way that they become mindfulness-supportive can in turn be related to a dimension of mindfulness itself. This dimension appears frequently in the early discourses, which distinguish between mindfulness applied internally and externally. Although the meaning of this distinction is not fully spelled out and later traditions have presented a range of different perspectives on the implications of internal and external mindfulness, it seems fair to assume that this applies to being mindful of what happens within ourselves, *internally*, and what takes place with others and therefore, from our viewpoint, *externally* (see Anālayo 2003b: 94–102, 2013: 17f, 2018f: 1970f, 2018i: 35–40, 2020b, and 2020d: 234f).

The impact of being mindful of the internal and external dimensions of our actions can be conveniently illustrated with the example of killing. As briefly mentioned above, this is the first of the five precepts usually taken by those who fully pledge themselves to following the Buddha's teachings as lay disciples (monastics take additional precepts, including celibacy). Carrying out an act of killing becomes much more difficult when we cultivate mindfulness externally, by bringing awareness to how killing affects the victim. This broadening of perspective prevents us focusing only on whatever reasons might motivate our wish to kill. Instead, with external mindfulness we increasingly learn to take into account the external repercussions of what we do to others.

In the case of killing in particular, this can lead to a substantial shift of perspective. In line with such a broadening of perspective, the discourses recommend reflecting that we do not want to be killed ourselves (Anālayo 2017g: 19). The same applies to others, who also do not want to be killed. Based on connecting our own preferences with those of others and developing empathy in this way, it becomes intolerable for us to inflict on others what we ourselves would certainly wish to avoid. How could we kill others, given that they wish to stay alive just as much as we do?

This basic reflection applies not only to killing, of course, but can be extended to a range of activities. The principle throughout is to expand our perspective and take into account both our own situation, the "internal", and that of others, the "external". It is based on such a broadening of perspective that the relevance and benefits of ethics will become naturally clear to us.

The deeper we become involved in the cultivation of mindfulness, the more we will notice the ethical repercussions of our actions. Due to the increased sensitivity to the results of our actions, it seems almost inevitable that sooner or later we will be motivated to improve and strengthen our moral conduct. In this way, ethical behaviour becomes something that grows together with our mindfulness practice.

RECOLLECTION OF MORALITY

Being established in moral conduct not only serves as a foundation for mindfulness, but can also become the object of mindfulness practice in the form of recollection. In this way, our mindfulness practice can lead to a strengthening of our ethical foundation, and our improved moral conduct can in turn become the object of the mindful practice of recollection.

The practice of recollection as such relates to the memory dimension of mindfulness, briefly mentioned in the previous chapter. The basic idea of recollection of morality is to direct attention to our own ethical integrity as a source of inspiration. Such recollection appears in a standard list of six such practices, which take the following objects (see also Anālayo 2017g: 225–231 and 2020d: 17–20):

- the Buddha,
- the teaching proclaimed by the Buddha,
- the community of noble disciples of the Buddha,
- our own accomplishment in morality,
- our own accomplishment in generosity,
- our own accomplishment in qualities that are similar to those of celestial beings.

In the case of recollecting our own morality, the main object of the practice is our present level of moral integrity. Such recollection can generate joy and thereby encourage our commitment to keep improving our ethical conduct. All it takes is a moment of looking within, noting that the behaviour we have adopted is neither harmful for others nor ourselves. The basic procedure is to acknowledge mindfully both our failures and successes, and after such honest assessment take our successes as a reason for rejoicing. This is not an encouragement to turn a blind eye on moral lapses. However, instead of focusing on these lapses and berating ourselves, we can use the wholesome joy of inspiration in good ethical conduct as the main driving force for empowering our own moral uplift.

The practice of making morality a source of joyful recollection sets the appropriate framework for a genuine desire to keep strengthening our ethical foundation. It simply works much better than making feelings of guilt and obedience to a higher authority the mainstay of ethical practice. In the words of Ajahn Amaro (2015: 68), in this way

> the approach toward ethics is more pragmatic than dogmatic, it shifts the perspective from telling people what they should do to that of helping us to do ourselves and others a favor … there is no external authority that condemns or rewards; instead … this approach shifts the responsibility for well-being firmly into the individual's own hands.

In short, we can shift from a guilt-driven morality to a joy-based ethics, which can suffuse all aspects of our behaviour such that it becomes supportive of mindfulness. Undertaken in this way, ethical conduct as the foundation for mindfulness practice can bring an additional benefit by serving as a subject for the practice of recollection.

SUMMARY

Ethical conduct is an indispensable foundation for mindfulness practice aimed at liberation. The need for such a firm foundation does not hold to the same degree when mindfulness is used for more mundane purposes, such as improvement of health. Nevertheless, genuine mindfulness practice will sooner or later have an impact on our ethical sensitivity and naturally lead to the wish to improve our moral standards.

Of particular help to ethics can be a directing of mindfulness to the external, in addition to the internal, by noting how others are affected by what we do. This complements mindfulness cultivated internally, in the sense of monitoring what happens within us. Both modes of mindfulness in combination lead to a full apperception of what is happening and thereby improve our ability to interact with others skilfully and harmoniously. Maintaining moral conduct in this way as an integral part of mindfulness practice can in turn serve as an object for mindful recollection.

The exploration in this chapter points in particular to the breadth of vision gained when mindfulness is applied both internally and externally. This reflects a basic quality of broadmindedness as an important dimension of mindfulness, comparable to a broad-angled lens for taking a picture. The resultant comprehensive vision of any situation is not only richer in detail, but also sees how things interrelate with each other and thereby contextualizes them. In contrast to narrow-mindedness and self-centredness, this dimension of mindfulness fosters open-mindedness and to some degree naturally nurtures an empathic concern for others. To the topic of compassion I turn in the next chapter.

PRACTICE SUGGESTIONS

A practical suggestion related to this chapter would be to explore the external dimension of mindfulness in daily life. Such exploration builds on our basic familiarity with mindfulness directed internally through the practice of mindful eating. It also continues the trend of gradually introducing mindfulness into our lives in ways that do not require setting apart special times and places.

The task of external mindfulness is simply to explore to what extent we can increase our awareness of how our actions affect others. This can be determined not only by what others explicitly communicate to us, but also by observing their tone of voice, facial expression, and bodily posture. Any effort invested in such practice will quickly pay off in enhancing our ability to communicate and interrelate with others more effectively and more harmoniously.

In addition, mindfulness practice could also be gradually applied to specific routine activities. For example, for some days we might try to see how it feels when we are fully mindful while getting up in the morning or going to bed at night. Next, we might try to introduce mindfulness to our daily toothbrushing.

All of this can be done in a spirit of playful exploration; it can become a kind of personal research conducted in order to see for ourselves what difference mindfulness can make.

Based on the foundation laid in this way in our own experience, we can come to appreciate how aspects of our daily routine and life might be made more mindfulness-supportive. We can also learn to identify ways of behaving which protect us from becoming stressed, distracted, and out of touch with ourselves. Being out of touch with ourselves typically happens when we revert to autopilot mode while doing a particular activity. Whenever we notice this, we can investigate if there might be alternatives to such habitual behaviour, if in some way or another we can apply mindfulness to improve our well-being and enliven these areas of our life. In this way, we gradually learn to become more alive, more in touch within and without, and increasingly more mindful.

III

MINDFULNESS AND COMPASSION

Following up on the external dimensions of mindfulness, explored in the previous chapter, in this chapter I turn to the relationship between mindfulness and compassion. I begin by surveying the nature of compassion as described in the early Buddhist discourses. Then I examine the relationship between compassion and mindfulness. My next topic is the need for a foundation in mindfulness practice in order to be able to engage in the compassionate activity of teaching others. In the last part of this chapter, I examine the meditative cultivation of compassion and compare the practice of mindfulness to the cultivation of *mettā*.

EARLY BUDDHIST COMPASSION

The cultivation of compassion in early Buddhist meditation practice comes with a clear-cut ethical undercurrent, which connects it with the topics taken up in the preceding chapter. Put briefly, compassion is rooted in the intention for non-harm (Anālayo 2017e: 86f). The cultivation of compassion thereby directly stands in contrast to intentionally harming others or acting cruelly, let alone killing another. Building on a firm foundation of such moral restraint, compassion goes further. It does so by reaching out to those who are afflicted, motivated by the wish to help and protect them, under the overarching aspiration for the absence of any harm. Firmly rooted in the intention for non-harm, the beautiful flower of compassion blossoms.

Given that the main thrust of compassion is about preventing harm to anyone, in the case of King Pasenadi, taken up in Chapter 1, compassion would find its expression in the Buddha's reaction on seeing the king in his deplorable condition. With the intention of helping the king to cease his harmful behaviour, the Buddha gave him a suitable teaching. The teaching was motivated by compassion, but it did not include instructions on compassion. Instead, it was just about mindfulness.

Nevertheless, compassion in general stands in a close relationship with mindfulness, in particular its external application. It is precisely through an increased sensitivity to the way others are affected by what we do, as an outcome of mindfulness directed externally, that we will naturally be motivated to try our best to avoid harming them. Out of a sustained cultivation of external mindfulness, compassion almost inevitably arises.

In some later Buddhist traditions, the implications of compassion change, evident in an emphasis on taking the pain of others onto oneself (Anālayo 2017e). This relates to a shift in perspective of the ultimate goal of a Buddhist practitioner, which by then had turned into the aspiration to become a Buddha oneself. Those who have such an aspiration follow the path of a "bodhisattva", one who is in quest of Buddhahood. Since a Buddha is a rather extraordinary person, this path requires considerably more preparation and effort than the noble eightfold path of early Buddhism, aimed simply at liberation from craving and attachment.

Compassion became the central motivation for undertaking this path of a bodhisattva towards becoming a Buddha, one who is able to discover the way to liberation and then teach it to others. To fortify followers of the bodhisattva path against the temptation of giving up their lofty aspiration, in some traditions compassion became increasingly related to empathically feeling the pain and distress of others who are immersed in suffering. The rationale was that one's resolve to follow the long and arduous path to future Buddhahood will be strengthened if the suffering of others is experienced as one's own.

Early Buddhist compassion, however, is not about trying to feel the suffering of others, which inevitably afflicts the one who practises in this way. Instead of being a painful experience, the cultivation of early Buddhist compassion leads to joy and happiness, while at the same time remaining rooted in an overall emphasis on the quality of non-harm. Such compassion can take the form of aspiring and endeavouring for those immersed in suffering to become free of it. Such sincere wishing for others to be free from harm and affliction then becomes the central motivational force for taking the appropriate action to achieve that aim. This aspiration, although clearly recognizing the suffering of others, does not dwell on the actual affliction but instead focuses on the prospect of others being free from harm and pain. By taking this reference point, such compassion can become a joyful experience.

THE RELATIONSHIP BETWEEN COMPASSION AND MINDFULNESS

As mentioned briefly in the previous chapter, based on the course set by the first path factor of right view, the second factor of the noble eightfold path is right intention. This second factor usually involves three types of intentions:

- renunciation in contrast to sensual indulgence,
- non-ill will in contrast to anger,
- non-harming in contrast to cruelty.

The first of these three, renunciation in contrast to sensual indulgence, could be related to the story of King Pasenadi, taken up in Chapter 1. Through being mindful while eating, he overcame his tendency to indulge in the sensual pleasure of overeating. This can be considered a practical application of the intention of renunciation.

The second type of intention, non-ill will in contrast to anger, relates to the quality of loving kindness or benevolence, also known by the Pāli term *mettā*. This quality is the direct opposite of anger and ill will. In the early discourses, *mettā* is mentioned more frequently than compassion and can be seen as laying a foundation of kindness in various dimensions of daily conduct, out of which compassion grows.

The last of these three types of intention, non-harming in contrast to cruelty, is in turn a direct reflection of compassion. This type of intention implicitly places compassion within the framework of the noble eightfold path, in the sense that non-harming, so central in the early Buddhist conception of compassion, is part of the path factor of right intention.

Among the three types of intention, the first is rather distinct from the other two, as non-ill will and non-harming seem closely related. Perhaps it is precisely because of the importance of avoiding both ill will and harming that these have been mentioned separately, rather than being combined into a single type of intention.

Just as ill will or anger has a considerable overlap with

harming but is not identical with it, so *mettā* and compassion have considerable overlap but are not identical. They differ in subtle ways in the attitude they generate. In the early discourses, *mettā* and compassion are both directed to all living beings, showing that they can take the same object. Clearly the distinction between these two cannot be related to their recipients (such as by assuming that compassion is simply *mettā* directed to those who are suffering). Instead, the difference lies in their actual disposition. In particular, *mettā* or benevolence takes the form of cultivating the attitude of being a friend to whomever we meet, whereas compassion comes with a special emphasis on avoiding any possible hurt or injury.

In addition to the factors of the noble eightfold path already examined in the previous chapter, the cultivation of the four establishments of mindfulness in turn forms the seventh factor of this path. This is preceded by the sixth path factor of right effort, in the sense of making an exertion to overcome harmful mental states and to cultivate those that are beneficial. The factor of right mindfulness is followed by the eighth and last factor of this path, which is right concentration. This stands for the mental tranquillity and composure, the inner stillness and happiness that are reached by cultivating the first seven factors of the eightfold path (Anālayo 2019c). Here are the eight factors again, for ease of consultation:

1) right view
2) right intention
3) right speech
4) right action
5) right livelihood
6) right effort
7) right mindfulness
8) right concentration

In this way compassion, together with *mettā*, are central dimensions of the right intention (2) that informs the eightfold path. Behind this right intention stands the diagnostic scheme of the four noble truths in the form of right view (1). Mindfulness cultivated by way of the four establishments of mindfulness (7) in turn is a central dimension of the meditative implementation of the path. This has its foundation in the preceding factors of mindfulness-supportive ethical behaviour in the domains of speech (3), action (4), and livelihood (5), and the factor of improving the ethical quality of one's mind through right effort (6). Mindfulness in turn leads on to the gaining of concentration (8).

PRACTICE AND TEACHING

Another dimension of the relationship between compassion and mindfulness emerges when engaging in teaching mindfulness to others, motivated by the compassionate concern for their well-being and freedom from harm. Serving as a competent instructor in mindfulness requires not only a compassionate motivation, but also needs building a foundation in ethics and, of course, cultivating mindfulness itself. In fact, personal practice of mindfulness is indispensable. This can be illustrated with the help of a simile found in the discourses, according to which it is impossible for one who is drowning to pull out another who is in the same predicament (see Anālayo 2020d: 188). To pull out another who is drowning is only possible if we make sure we are not drowning ourselves. Similarly, the discourse continues, in order to train another in a particular quality, we need to establish ourselves in this quality first. This should be as plainly evident as the need to be standing on firm ground when wanting to pull out another from a quagmire.

The discourse applies this principle to a range of qualities, one of which is mindfulness. The relevant passage indicates that those who lack mindfulness can overcome this deficiency by establishing mindfulness. In other words, if we lack mindfulness, this needs to be addressed first, and only then are we really ready to act out our compassionate motivation and teach mindfulness to others.

This basic principle relates to a distinction made in the discourses that is directly relevant to the theme of compassion. The teaching in question takes up four types of persons, distinguished according to whether they benefit themselves or others. Out of these, those who benefit both are reckoned the best and those who benefit neither the worst of the four. Surprisingly, however, those who benefit only themselves are reckoned superior to those who benefit only others (Anālayo 2017e: 85f). The reasoning behind this presentation is that those of the first type at least practise themselves, whereas those in the second group only tell others to practise, without doing so themselves.

This in turn sets a context for the cultivation of mindfulness and compassion in early Buddhism, in the sense that the wish to help others emerge from harm should not cause one to neglect one's own practice. Moreover, it endows cultivating good qualities like mindfulness with a compassionate potential. It is precisely such cultivation which gradually builds up the ability to help others who are sinking in the mud of suffering and distress.

THE MEDITATIVE PRACTICE OF COMPASSION

References to compassion in the Pāli discourses actually involve two distinct terms. One of these is used primarily for compassionate action, whereas the other usually refers to the meditative cultivation of compassion (Anālayo 2015a: 13). These two dimensions of compassion mutually strengthen each other.

The meditative cultivation of compassion is part of a set of four mental attitudes, which comprise also *mettā* (usually translated as "loving kindness"), sympathetic joy, and equanimity. These are collectively known as "divine abodes" or alternatively as being states of mind that are "boundless". The notion of a divine abode can be taken to reflect their elevating and sublime nature, leading the practitioner to an inner condition that is like being in heaven.

The qualification of boundlessness in turn can be related to the predominant mode of meditative cultivation described in the early discourses. This meditative cultivation takes the form of a radiation of compassion (or any of the other three) in all directions (see Anālayo 2015a: 20–26 and 54–57 and 2015b: 9–22). The approach of directing *mettā* or compassion to a friend, a neutral person, and an enemy, common in later tradition, is not found in this form in the early discourses and reflects later developments (Anālayo 2015b and 2019g). The boundless mental condition described in the early discourses can also eventually be reached using this later approach, after the meditator has again dissolved the distinctions between friend, neutral person, and an enemy. Seen from this perspective, although they involve somewhat different modes of practice, the two models of cultivation converge on the boundless nature of compassion (or *mettā*, etc.), once it has been well established.

METTĀ AND MINDFULNESS

At times, descriptions of the cultivation of *mettā* in the Pāli discourses come with a reference to mindfulness (see Anālayo 2019g: 2626). At the same time, however, mindfulness and *mettā* (or for that matter compassion) are different qualities in early Buddhist thought. Mindfulness is not considered to be invariably an ethically positive quality. This is evident in references to "wrong" forms of mindfulness, the opposite of right mindfulness as the seventh factor of the noble eightfold path. The recognition of these two opposed modes implies that mindfulness can at times manifest in an ethically negative form.

In contrast, *mettā* and compassion are ethically positive. There is no "wrong" *mettā* or compassion, because types of love and affection that run counter to the path to awakening are designated with other terms, not with those used for *mettā* and compassion. Moreover, *mettā* and compassion are more specific meditative themes, whereas mindfulness can be related to a whole range of meditative topics, such as the breath, for example, or one's own mortality, or recollection of the Buddha, etc.

At the same time, there is some overlap between the cultivation of *mettā* or compassion and the practice of mindfulness. This overlap can be found in the experience of boundlessness. *Mettā* and compassion become boundless by dint of being free from any limit, by not excluding anyone in any direction from their benevolent and altruistic disposition. Mindfulness becomes boundless once internal and external cultivation, discussed in the previous chapter, lead to the flourishing of openness and breadth of mind, which similarly can come to be without limit. In fact, several discourses explicitly qualify certain types of mindfulness practice as leading to a "boundless" mental condition, a topic I will explore in more detail in the next chapter. In this way, the theme of boundlessness and the absence of limits can be considered as a converging point of the cultivation of *mettā* or compassion and the practice of mindfulness.

SUMMARY

Compassion in early Buddhism is primarily rooted in the intention for the absence of harm; it does not require taking unto oneself the pain of others. As one of three aspects of right intention, compassion is firmly built into the noble eightfold path as part of the setting within which the cultivation of the path factor of right mindfulness takes place. The compassionate activity of teaching mindfulness to others requires first of all establishing ourselves in this quality, thereby learning to embody what we wish to instil in others. The cultivation of compassion and the practice of mindfulness converge on a boundless condition of the mind that has gone beyond the creating of barriers and the imposing of limits.

PRACTICE SUGGESTIONS

Practice suggestions for this chapter continue in line with the two previous chapters by attempting to relate directly to daily life, without a need to set aside a special time or place for meditation practice. Over the course of the next set of three chapters, this approach will gradually change, as other aspects of mindfulness practice do require setting aside time and space for formal meditation. Needless to say, the cultivation of compassion (and *mettā*) can benefit considerably from being undertaken as a formal sitting practice.

Exploring daily-life applications can build on the cultivation of external mindfulness, introduced in the previous chapter. An increased awareness of how our actions affect others can lead over to meeting them with the open heart of compassion, as an expression of our sincere intention for non-harm. Whenever we are able to arouse such an attitude of compassion, we might take a moment to notice the expansiveness of the mind that results from being in this condition. The mind can become spacious when we just stop creating borders and defending them. In contrast, if we become angry or cruel, the mind becomes narrow and confined. Noticing the remarkable difference between these two conditions of our own mind makes it intuitively clear why the boundless condition is preferable; why compassion benefits not only others, but also ourselves.

All it takes is to arouse a sincere aspiration for non-harm and dwell in the resultant condition of the mind. This can then manifest in a variety of expressions in daily life, from taking care of the weak and feeble to sharing our possessions and time with those in need or giving encouragement and support to those who require it. All of these actions can become expressions of our compassion.

IV

EMBODIED MINDFULNESS

The meditative cultivation of *mettā* and compassion, examined in the last chapter, can lead to a boundless mental state, a quality the discourses also apply to mindfulness of the body. In order to explore this particular modality of mindfulness, I begin this chapter by surveying different meditative attitudes towards the body in early Buddhist thought in general. Then I turn to similes that illustrate mindfulness of the body and explore the topic of sense restraint. Another simile featuring a cowherd leads me to consider the contrast between right and wrong forms of mindfulness.

THE BODY IN EARLY BUDDHIST MEDITATION

Mindfulness of the body is the topic of one particular discourse, appropriately called the Discourse on Mindfulness of the Body (see Anālayo 2020d: 68–81). The different practices presented in this discourse conveniently exemplify a range of perspectives on the body in early Buddhist meditation (Anālayo 2017c: 43–63).

One of these exercises concerns the anatomical constitution of the body. It requires discerning that in our own body there are such bodily parts as hair, skin, flesh, bones, various organs, liquids, etc. The instructions come with an explicit element of evaluation, indicating that the body should be regarded as not attractive or not clean. The exercise is clearly meant to lead to an attitude of disengaging ourselves from any attachment to, or infatuation with, the body as a means of sensual gratification (Anālayo 2003b: 146–149, 2013: 63–80, and 2018i: 47–63).

The Discourse on Mindfulness of the Body also clarifies the purpose of cultivating such an attitude, which is to facilitate the mind becoming quiet and concentrated. The logic behind this is that yearning for sensual gratification inevitably results in an incessant search for something alluring, which prevents the mind from settling down internally. Yet, if the mind were to settle down, forms of happiness and joy could be experienced that are vastly superior to anything that sensual gratification could ever yield.

These instructions are found not only in the Discourse on Mindfulness of the Body, but also in the Discourse on the Establishments of Mindfulness. In both cases, it is worth noting that the exercise itself does not refer to mindfulness at all (Anālayo 2013: 36f and 2018i: 43f). The actual instructions are to "examine" the body in a certain way, and such an examination then becomes one of several ways to "contemplate" the body.

Mindfulness is of course relevant throughout all the practices described in both discourses, but the actual evaluation is not something intrinsic to mindfulness itself. Rather, it pertains to a specific cognitive training to counter sensuality, a training for which mindfulness just furnishes the component of presence of the mind.

A contrast to the somewhat negative attitude towards the body, evident in the instructions for contemplating the body's anatomical parts, can be found in another exercise in the same discourse that relates to deep states of concentration. Early Buddhist thought regularly mentions four levels of such concentrative "absorption". The Discourse on Mindfulness of the Body takes up each of these four from the viewpoint of their embodied experience (see Anālayo 2011: 673f and 2020d: 72–75).

Already with the experience of the first absorption, for example, the practitioner experiences a thorough pervasion of the whole body with joy and happiness. This finds illustration in the example of soap powder that is thoroughly mixed and saturated with water. The bodily experience of the second absorption is compared to water that is welling up from below. The somatic dimension of the third absorption is likened to a lotus completely submerged in water, and the imperturbable condition reached with the fourth absorption is compared to a person being completely covered by a cloth. Such descriptions of embodied bliss and ease are the very opposite of a deprecation of the body (Anālayo 2017c: 56–60).

Mindfulness in its function of monitoring what happens within the mind is an important aid in cultivating these absorptions. As a quality present during each of the four absorptions (Anālayo 2019k), it serves to maintain mental presence in the midst of the experience of fully embodied joy and happiness, as well as embodied equanimity, maintaining the mind in its balanced and concentrated condition. In such contexts, mindfulness does not function in isolation. Instead, it operates in collaboration with other mental factors, in particular with concentration.

Another exercise mentioned in the Discourse on Mindfulness of the Body, also for the purpose of leading to stillness of the mind and concentration, relates to mapping the spatial placement of the body by way of its main postures of walking, standing, sitting, and lying down (see Anālayo 2020d: 68–70). This mode of practice can be seen as a middle ground between the two modalities discussed above, with the evaluation of the anatomical nature of the body on the one end and fully embodied bliss on the other.

Contemplation of the four postures involves neither a deconstruction of the body as the counterbalance to sensual indulgence nor the somatic experience of absorption. It simply requires being mindfully present with the body in whatever posture this may be. The practice relies to some degree on "proprioceptive awareness", the ability to know the posture of our own body.

SIMILES ON MINDFULNESS OF THE BODY

The cultivation of mindfulness of the body finds illustration in several similes. One of these describes a person who has to carry a bowl full to the brim with oil. Given that in ancient India things were usually carried on the head, it seems safe to assume that the person is carrying the bowl on the head. This act of carrying is challenging for two reasons. One of these is that the person has to carry that bowl through a crowd which is watching a singing and dancing performance. This already quite distracting situation is further complicated by the fact that the carrier of the oil is followed by someone else with a sword, who is ready to cut off the carrier's head should any of the oil be spilled (see Anālayo 2003b: 122, 2013: 56f, 2018i: 20f, and 2020d: 57–62).

Executing this task would require keeping mindfulness well established on what is happening at the bodily level. Attention needs to be given to the inner sense of bodily balance while carrying the bowl. However, this should not result in an exclusive focus on the body, as staying attuned to inner bodily balance is complemented by needing to beware of others who might get in the way. Members of the crowd might suddenly step forward or be moving in rhythm with the singing. Any unnoticed movement by a member of the crowd can potentially cause jostling or stumbling. Moreover, there is the need to avoid becoming distracted by the dancing and singing performance itself. Being followed by the other person with a sword at the ready, there is no scope for allowing distraction from the task at hand to occur even for a moment.

This rather dramatic description conveys the potential of rooting ourselves in postural awareness, in cultivating an embodied form of mindfulness. It points to a grounding quality of mindfulness. Out of the modalities of mindfulness of the body surveyed above, it relates in particular to postural awareness.

The practice of mindfulness of the body finds illustration in another simile, which describes six different animals, each bound with a length of rope to the same post which is firmly embedded in the ground. These animals represent the five sense experiences of seeing, hearing, smelling, tasting, and touching, together with the mind as a sixth sense. In the simile, each of these animals pulls in a different direction. Because of being bound to the post, however, they are unable to go wherever they wish to go (see Anālayo 2003b: 123, 2013: 55f, 2018i: 20, and 2020d: 62–65).

The image of six animals that want to go in different directions illustrates the usual fragmentation of our experience, due to which the mind tends to follow whatever happens to be the most prominent object for any of the senses. In our present-day situation, with mass communications and the whole variety of distractions available, this imagery is all the more pertinent.

The solution is to establish a firm anchor within, through mindfulness of the body. With mindfulness of the body established, it will become possible to remain centred, regardless of what happens at any sense-door. In addition to the grounding and centring dimension evident in the previous simile of carrying a bowl of oil, the image of the post to which six animals are bound points to the protective aspect of mindfulness of the body. In the simile of the bowl, mindfulness of the body served to protect the carrier of the oil from having the head cut off. The present simile brings this quality down from a rather dramatic and somewhat unrealistic situation directly into our everyday experience of fragmentation, due to being pulled along by one of our senses. In order to protect ourselves from being the hapless victims of such fragmentation and its inevitable detrimental impact on our mind, mindfulness of the body offers a way of meeting sensory input without getting carried away by it.

The practice of mindfulness of the body as a means to remain centred amidst various sense inputs can lead to a "boundless" mental state. As mentioned earlier, this is the same qualification the discourses also employ for the cultivation of *mettā* and compassion. In this way, mindfulness of the body and the cultivation of *mettā* or compassion appear to converge in a broad state of mind free from barriers. In the case of *mettā* and compassion, the barriers are anger and cruelty; in the case of mindfulness of the body, the corresponding barrier would presumably be the fragmentation of experience due to being pulled along by one or another of the senses. Instead of such fragmentation, the mind can remain established in a more comprehensive wide-angle perspective. Within this breadth of mind, sensory information can be received without resulting in a narrowing down that focuses on just a single sense-door to the exclusion of anything else.

SENSE RESTRAINT

The simile of the six animals conveys the gist of a mode of practice that comes under the heading of "sense restraint" in early Buddhist thought. Sense restraint requires that we avoid clinging to the details of what has been perceived, or to its secondary characteristics, in the sense of associations called up by those details. These details are required in order for us to recognize things. It is with the help of such details, in the sense of distinctive features, that our perception is able to identify people we meet or things we see (Anālayo 2003a). But there is no need to cling to them.

Such sense restraint does not make us dysfunctional. In fact, the discourses regularly recommended that monastics practise sense restraint during their daily begging tour. In order to be able to notice when it is appropriate to stop walking during their tour to receive food or else to continue on, of course they need to be able to perceive whether someone is willing to make an offering. Thus the practice of sense restraint needs to be undertaken in such a way that it does not interfere with recognizing these type of details. Otherwise it would become self-defeating.

Sense restraint therefore only concerns avoiding any clutching at details that will lead to the arising of what the Buddhist traditions consider mental defilements. The instructions on sense restraint make this quite clear by explicitly mentioning that the overall purpose is the avoidance of unwholesome states like greedy desires or dejection. The same unwholesome qualities are also mentioned in the Discourse on the Establishments of Mindfulness, where a systematic cultivation of mindfulness serves to keep both at bay. This in turn points to a close relationship between mindfulness and sense restraint. Mindfulness is necessary to notice clearly what is taking place whenever the mind is taking in details of our sense experience that could trigger unwholesome reactions. This requires, in particular, mental receptivity through mindfulness. By remaining mindfully receptive to the external situation and its repercussions within our mind, we can learn to avoid unwholesome reactions.

THE COWHERD SIMILE

A simile that illustrates a receptive quality of mindfulness involves a cowherd in two distinct situations. In the first situation the crop is ripe and the cowherd has to watch the cows closely and actively prevent them from straying into the fields. In the second situation, however, the crop has been harvested and there is no longer any danger that the cows might eat it. In this situation, the cowherd just needs to be mindful of them (see Anālayo 2003b: 53, 2013: 147f, 2018i: 9–11, and 2020d: 171f).

Apart from needing to have a broad overview of where the cows are grazing, the second situation also conveys a flavour of non-interfering receptivity as a characteristic of mindfulness. This does not mean that mindfulness makes it impossible to take action when needed. The point is only that this dimension of non-interfering breadth of mind emerges when mindfulness is cultivated on its own.

In fact, the purpose of the simile in its original setting is to illustrate how to handle different types of thought. If thoughts of sensual lust, ill will, and cruelty manifest, an effort needs to be made to counteract them. This pertains to the domain of right effort, a factor of the path of practice that is distinct from the path factor of mindfulness. Such effort is similar to the cowherd's need to keep the cows away from the ripe crop. But with wholesome thoughts such effort is no longer needed. Similarly, once the crop has been harvested the cowherd can relax and adopt a more passive observational stance comparable to mindfulness practised on its own.

RIGHT AND WRONG MINDFULNESS

In addition to drawing out these nuances, the cowherd simile is also of interest in relation to another topic. This is the ethical quality of mindfulness, which I now take up briefly. As mentioned earlier, the discourses distinguish between "right" and "wrong" manifestations of mindfulness. Simply said, when mindfulness is practised as part of the noble eightfold path, it is of the right type. But when mindfulness leads in the direction opposite to this path, it is of the wrong type. If mindfulness is employed in such a way that it harms ourselves or others, if it leads to an increase in unwholesome qualities and a decrease of wholesome qualities, then such mindfulness should be reckoned as "wrong".

What about the cowherd's mindfulness? Such type of mindfulness is not part of a cultivation of the noble eightfold path. It does not seem to have any self-evident connection to this path and also does not really have a potential to lead to liberation. However much the cowherd may be mindful of the cows, this will not by itself result in awakening. At the same time, it also does not seem to be something that is diametrically opposed to the noble eightfold path or that increases unwholesome qualities. It seems simply to be unrelated to either of these two. In other words, there might be applications of mindfulness that fail to satisfy the criterion of being "right" but need not for that reason be categorized as "wrong".

SUMMARY

Early Buddhism offers a variety of perspectives on the body, which range from deconstructing the body's sensual allure to the embodied experience of deep bliss during meditative absorption. A fairly neutral mode of mindfulness practice involves awareness of bodily postures. Being rooted in mindfulness of the body can counter distraction through the senses and thereby the usual tendency to fragmentation of experience. Such potential reveals a grounding quality of mindfulness as well as a protective dimension. This in turn fosters non-reactivity to whatever happens, by way of not clinging to those details of sense objects that could trigger greedy desires or dejection. A distinctive aspect of mindfulness appears to be receptive non-interference, in the sense of observation free from active involvement. To contrast modalities of mindfulness as "right" or "wrong" does not seem to function as an exhaustive account of all possible manifestations of mindfulness, some of which might not fit smoothly either of these two categories.

PRACTICE SUGGESTIONS

The present chapter is the first of three chapters which gradually proceed to more formal meditation practices, based on some familiarity with mindfulness developed by applying it to daily-life situations, as presented in the previous three chapters. In line with those earlier practices, mindfulness could simply be applied to bodily activities that we already do on a regular basis. This could be cleaning our room, gardening, etc. With any of these activities, the task would be to perform them with our whole body, to be fully embodied when doing them and remain with mindfulness established.

Based on familiarity with joining mindfulness to embodiment, the same practice can then be applied to more formal meditation, such as walking meditation. For such practice, we could find an area where we can walk up and down or in a circle without being interrupted or distracted by others. We start by just standing, feeling our whole body and establishing the presence of mindfulness. Then we walk at whatever speed seems suitable to us. This could be slow-motion walking or else walking at normal speed. Throughout, whenever we notice that we have become distracted, we gently and softly come back to whole-body awareness, and thereby to being fully embodied in the here and now.

V

MINDFULNESS AND FOCUSED ATTENTION

In this chapter I investigate the relationship between mindfulness and focused attention (Anālayo 2020a). I begin by considering a recommendation in one discourse to shift from cultivating the establishments of mindfulness to another type of meditation practice in order to concentrate the mind. This mode of presentation implies that these two approaches to meditation are not identical, otherwise there would have been no need to shift from the one to the other. From this discourse I then proceed to explore the practice of mindfulness of breathing in sixteen steps. The meditative dynamics inherent in this meditative progression appear to have been lost sight of in later times, promoting a tendency to focus on the breath. I then turn to another relevant development in the Theravāda tradition in particular, which led to understanding mindfulness as a quality of plunging into the object of the mind.

COUNTERING DISTRACTION

A central purpose of cultivating focused attention is to counter the mind's ingrained tendency to distraction. The arising of distraction during mindfulness practice is the theme of a discourse which begins with a group of nuns who report their successful cultivation of the four establishments of mindfulness to the Buddha's attendant Ānanda (see Anālayo 2020d: 107–110). This confirms a point made in Chapter 2 that, even though instructions on mindfulness are regularly addressed to "monks", they were neither the sole recipients of such instructions nor the only ones who successfully put them into practice (see above p. 20).

On being informed by Ānanda of the nuns' practice, the Buddha offers further advice on how to cultivate the four establishments of mindfulness so as to be similarly successful. He takes the case of someone who experiences sluggishness or is distracted outwardly while cultivating mindfulness. In such a case, the advice is to shift to another form of practice. This mode of practice should be one that inspires and engenders joy, tranquillity, happiness, and concentration. These mental conditions are part of a recurrent description in the discourses, according to which the arousing of wholesome types of joy and happiness (wholesome in the sense of not being related to sensuality) enhances the ability to concentrate the mind.

The discourse on the nuns' practice continues with the reflection that, once concentration has been gained in this way, the purpose of taking up another practice has been fulfilled and it is now possible to return to the cultivation of the four establishments of mindfulness. The Pāli discourse introduces specific terminology to distinguish these two modes of meditation: using something inspiring is a "directed" form of mental cultivation whereas the practice of mindfulness can be considered an "undirected" form of mental cultivation.

This distinction concords well with what emerges from other passages concerning mindfulness, some of which I discussed in previous chapters. These give the impression that a conspicuous dimension of mindfulness is an open receptivity, a non-interfering mental attitude. Needless to say, some degree of mindfulness also needs to be present when attending to an inspiring theme in order to cultivate the type of joy and happiness that leads to concentration. Mindfulness is such a versatile quality that it can be combined with a range of other mental conditions and meditative practices. At the same time, the above Pāli discourse does give the impression that mindfulness on its own has more of an "undirected" character.

This impression needs to be evaluated further in relation to instructions on mindfulness of breathing. This modality of meditation practice is often taught and practised with a strong emphasis on focusing on the breath to the exclusion of anything else, in order to prevent the mind becoming distracted. Such distraction is in itself only natural, given that the breath on its own is rather bland and uninteresting. Hence it might seem natural that a strong degree of effort is needed in order to keep the breath in mind. In order to explore this further, I now survey the relevant canonical instructions.

PRELIMINARIES TO MINDFULNESS OF BREATHING

The instructions on mindfulness of breathing given regularly in the early discourses begin by describing some preliminaries to formal sitting meditation. Since with the present chapter I introduce formal sitting meditation in my practice suggestions, it seems opportune to take a closer look at these preliminaries before examining the actual meditation on the breath. The relevant part of the Discourse on Mindfulness of Breathing (Anālayo 2019j: 6) proceeds as follows:

> Here gone to a forest or to the root of a tree or to an empty hut, one sits down; having folded the legs crosswise, keeping the body erect, and having established mindfulness to the fore, mindful one breathes in and mindful one breathes out.

The instructions describe retiring first of all to a secluded place. In the ancient Indian setting this would have been a forest, the root of a tree, or an empty hut. Applied to our personal living situation nowadays, the recommendation would be to try to find a place for formal sitting meditation that affords some seclusion and makes the occurrence of external disturbances less likely.

Folding the legs crosswise reflects the traditional meditation posture, which alternatively could also involve using a bench or a chair. The key aspect here is to offer the body a firm foundation so that it can relax, and to ensure that the back is kept straight. The need for "keeping the body erect" applies continuously for the remainder of the practice. This in turn would imply that some degree of whole-body awareness of the sitting posture is to be maintained. Based on this foundation in embodiment, mindfulness can be made a predominant quality in the mind, by coming "to the fore", as it were. With that established, we then breathe in and out with mindfulness.

The discourse continues by delineating sixteen steps of meditation practice that can be cultivated while remaining mindful of the distinction between breathing in and breathing out. It is worthy of note that these sixteen steps do not explicitly mention mindfulness, which only occurs in the part translated above. Although the reference here to mindfulness established "to the fore" allows for different interpretations, my personal suggestion would be to understand the phrase in the sense of making mindfulness predominant in the mind (Anālayo 2019j: 16). On this understanding, based on some degree of continuity of whole-body awareness to ensure that the back is kept straight, and with a state of mind in which mindfulness has become predominant, we attend to the process of breathing by discerning between inhalations and exhalations.

THE SIXTEEN STEPS OF MINDFULNESS OF BREATHING

Before surveying the sixteen steps, it deserves mention that the Buddha is on record for having experimented extensively with breath control when he was still in quest of awakening (Anālayo 2017g: 60–67). Later he abandoned such practice, finding it unconducive to progress towards awakening. Once having reached awakening and become a Buddha, the approach to the breath he taught to others was based on mindful observation instead of forceful control. The breath is simply to be watched with mindfulness, which is indeed the main mode of practice in the sixteen steps.

In the Discourse on Mindfulness of Breathing, these sixteen steps take place alongside continuous mindful observation of the ongoing process of inhalations and exhalations. Based on that continuity, the breaths should be discerned as either long or short. Next comes a shift to what appears to require a broadening of awareness from the breath to the body as a whole, followed by a calming of any bodily activity. This first set of meditative steps fulfils the first establishment of mindfulness, contemplation of the body.

The meditative progression in this first set of meditative steps involves a focus on the breath, in particular when having to discern whether the breath is long or short. Without some degree of close scrutiny and concentration on the breath itself, it will not be possible to determine its length. At the same time, however, this would have to be accompanied by at least a minimal amount of awareness of the bodily posture to prevent any slouching. Following the interpretation of these instructions that to my mind makes the most sense, the next step involves broadening awareness to encompass the whole body. This is then followed by calming bodily activity, both of which are observed alongside continuous awareness of the inhalations and exhalations.

The instructions continue by combining awareness of the breath with the experience of joy, happiness, and mental activity, followed by calming mental activity. These four meditative steps correspond to the second establishment of mindfulness, contemplation of feeling tones. The actual progression concords with a basic principle briefly mentioned above, in that the arousing of joy and happiness naturally leads to the mind becoming less distracted and more concentrated, which here eventually leads to a calming of mental activity. Each of these distinct meditative steps takes place while remaining aware of inhalations and exhalations.

With the continuity of such mindful observation of the process of breathing, next come the steps of experiencing, gladdening, concentrating, and liberating the mind. These four meditative steps, which continue a trajectory towards mental tranquillity already evident in the preceding set of four steps, correspond to the third establishment of mindfulness, contemplation of the mind.

The counterpart to the fourth establishment of mindfulness involves contemplating a variety of insight perspectives that build on awareness of impermanence. Here the experience of impermanence elicits dispassion, in the sense of a fading away of passion, and cessation, in particular of attachments, culminating in a profound inner letting go.

The meditative progression that emerges in this way does not seem to be confined to the breath alone. Some degree of focus is indeed needed at the outset when discerning the length of the breath as long or short. This has the function of providing an initial settling of the mind. The remainder of the practice, however, does not involve an exclusive focus. On the contrary, the need to maintain awareness of the inhalations and exhalations alongside each step of the whole progression is rather inclusive in nature. It is perhaps for this reason that the whole practice is termed "mindfulness" of breathing, rather than "focusing" on breathing.

In this way, based on an initial training in focus, the remainder of the practice unfolds in a more inclusive and open manner. The ability of the mind to avoid succumbing to distraction is fostered by establishing whole-body awareness and then arousing joy and happiness which, due to their pleasant nature, naturally strengthen the mind's ability to stay in the present. Based on these, the remainder of the progression can lead to deep levels of tranquillity and to maturing insight.

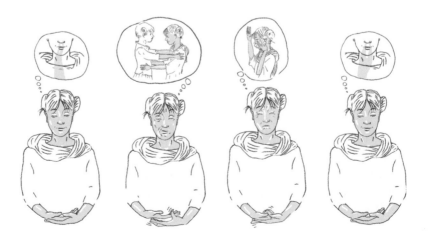

THE FIRST STEPS OF MINDFULNESS OF BREATHING

As part of an apparent tendency to bring together various practices related to contemplation of the body, the first few steps of mindfulness of breathing seem to have been taken out of their original context and integrated in the Discourse on Mindfulness of the Body and the Discourse on the Establishments of Mindfulness (Anālayo 2019j: 165). Although such integration is in itself quite understandable, the net result is that these first steps become isolated as a practice on their own.

Divorced from the dynamic that ensues with subsequent steps, in particular the experience of joy and happiness as means to generate concentration, mindfulness of breathing reduced to its first few steps no longer has the same potential. This holds especially for a benefit mentioned regularly in the discourse, namely the potential to overcome mental distraction.

As a result of being left to achieve this benefit using only the first few steps, a tendency to cultivate a strong degree of focus is only natural. This could well have contributed to the arising of meditative approaches that involve counting the breaths. Such a practice, which is not found in the early discourses, appears to have gained widespread acceptance and become prevalent in various Buddhist traditions. The idea is to relate each breath to a count, perhaps from one to ten, and then start over again (Anālayo 2019j: 232). Although such counting must have considerable benefits, given that it has found such widespread appeal, it does seem to differ considerably from the approach to breath meditation reflected in the early discourses.

MINDFULNESS AND MENTAL FLOATING

Already with the development depicted above, a closer association of focused attention with mindfulness practice (here mindfulness of breathing) can be discerned. The same tendency appears to have been further fuelled by a particular term (*apilāpana*) that in the Theravāda exegetical tradition had become part of a list of synonyms for mindfulness (see below p. 114). As a result, mindfulness eventually came to be understood as a quality that plunges into whatever the mind takes as its objects.

The idea of plunging into the object further reinforces the association of mindfulness with focused attention. Rather than being a receptive and non-interfering quality that stands back and allows things to unfold within a broad field of awareness, with this understanding mindfulness comes to be invested with quite an active and even almost aggressive nuance.

Noting this development is not meant to imply that mindfulness in early Buddhist meditation could not coexist with focus. The point is only that, in such contexts, mindfulness cooperates with another mental quality. In a way, mindfulness could be compared to water, which can either be used on its own or else combined with other ingredients to make a soup. Even though both types of usage involve water, the resultant flavour is quite different. Comparable to plain water, mindfulness on its own appears to be more a receptive form of awareness characterized by breadth of mind rather than narrow focus. In contrast to the exclusive nature of a strong focus, according to Gunaratana (1991/1992: 165) "mindfulness is inclusive. It stands back from the focus of attention and watches with a broad focus." The quality of breadth of mind became evident in the last chapter in relation to mindfulness of the body, which the discourses explicitly relate to a boundless mental condition.

SUMMARY

The experience of distraction when cultivating the four establishments of mindfulness can be countered by shifting to another meditation practice that inspires and thereby leads to the arousing of joy and happiness, engendering concentration. The potential of joy and happiness in this respect is evident in the instructions on mindfulness of breathing in sixteen steps. In later times, an emphasis on only the first steps of these instructions appears to have led to losing sight of the potential of joy and happiness to counter the mind's tendency to distraction.

Mindfulness of breathing came to be associated with a stronger focus on the breath, supported by additional techniques like counting the breaths. A misunderstanding or re-interpretation of a particular term in the Theravāda tradition led to the idea that mindfulness plunges into its object. In this way, the element of focused attention appears to have gained increasing weight over other, more inclusive qualities of mindfulness. Appreciating this development requires bearing in mind that mindfulness can collaborate with various other factors of the mind, including focused attention. At the same time, a strong focus is not an intrinsic quality of mindfulness itself.

PRACTICE SUGGESTIONS

For actual practice, I would suggest employing the preliminaries to mindfulness of breathing, translated above. Although the full potential of mindfulness of breathing emerges with the whole scheme of sixteen steps, for the time being it seems appropriate to begin with the basic practice of just being mindful of the breath.

Becoming aware of the breath could in principle be applied to various daily situations. On such an understanding, the present practice could still be placed in a continuum with the emphasis in previous chapters on integrating mindfulness in various ways with what we are already doing. Yet, the instructions translated above recommend finding a secluded place and sitting down for meditation, so my suggestion would be to make this as much a formal practice as possible within our current living situation. In future chapters the breath will appear repeatedly as a tool to explore various other meditative perspectives on mindfulness, some of which are quite subtle and thus do require the support formal sitting can provide.

In relation to the topic of the present chapter, it would be best to be mindful of inhalations and exhalations without turning this into an exercise in exclusive focus. This can be achieved by allowing the breath to be part of whole-body awareness, a modality of mindfulness already introduced in the last chapter.

Although the breath can at times stand out quite prominently and distinctly, nevertheless, this should not lead to forgetting about the rest of the body completely.

In terms of the actual physical location where we observe the breath, different meditators find diverse approaches useful. Some like the nose tip or the upper lip, others inside the throat, the chest, or the abdomen. Others, including myself, prefer not to rely on any particular physical location. Whatever appears to work best for us can be adopted for establishing mindfulness on the process of breathing. In order to take advantage of the potential of wholesome forms of joy and happiness, discussed above, whenever feasible the mindful experience of the breath could be accompanied by noting the pleasantness of the present condition of our body and mind, as they become increasingly quiet. Such noting can eventually lead to the spontaneous arising of wholesome types of joy, which substantially support our ability to remain mindfully aware of the inhalations and exhalations as they occur in the here and now.

VI

MINDFULNESS AND WISDOM

In what follows I examine the question of how mindfulness relates to the cultivation of wisdom, in particular by exploring the basic formula of the four establishments of mindfulness (*satipaṭṭhāna*). I begin by considering the monitoring aspect of mindfulness. This finds an expression in the circumstance that the basic formula repeats the domain of each establishment of mindfulness. In the case of the body, for example, this repetition takes the form of contemplating the body "in regard to the body".

The same basic formula for the establishments of mindfulness also points to a collaboration of mindfulness with other qualities: diligence and clear knowing. The latter is particularly relevant to the main topic of this chapter, the relationship between mindfulness and wisdom.

THE FOUR ESTABLISHMENTS OF MINDFULNESS

The practice surveyed in the previous chapter gave a first impression of the four establishments of mindfulness, as they correspond to the four sets of four steps in the instructions on sixteen steps of mindfulness of breathing. Their practice is not confined to the breath, however. A detailed survey of these four establishments can be found in the Discourse on the

Establishments of Mindfulness (Anālayo 2003b, 2013, and 2018i). This discourse lists a variety of ways to put into practice what are sometimes also called the four "foundations of mindfulness", a common rendering of the term *satipaṭṭhāna* that does not seem to capture the meaning as well as the term "establishment of mindfulness" (Anālayo 2003b: 29f). To illustrate the range of practices, here is a survey of the contemplations found in the Pāli version of the Discourse on the Establishments of Mindfulness:

First establishment:
• the first four steps of mindfulness of breathing,
• the bodily postures,
• clear comprehension in relation to various physical activities,
• the anatomical constitution of the body,
• the body as made up of the four material elements,
• a corpse in various stages of decay.

Second establishment:
• the three feeling tones, distinguished further into worldly and unworldly.

Third establishment:
• different states of mind.

Fourth establishment:
• five mental states that specifically hinder the proper functioning of the mind,
• five aspects of subjective experience we tend to cling to,
• the fettering force of experience through the six senses,
• seven mental qualities that lead to awakening,
• the four noble truths.

Text-critical study makes it fairly probable that some of these exercises are later additions to the Discourse on the Establishments of Mindfulness (Anālayo 2013). What remains as likely early elements of the first establishment of mindfulness are three body contemplations. One of these is examination of the anatomical constitution of the body as being made up of such parts as skin, hair, various organs and bodily liquids, etc., a form of practice already mentioned in Chapter 4 (see above p. 37). Another contemplation of the body involves the four material elements of earth, water, fire, and wind (representing the experiential qualities of solidity, cohesion, temperature, and motion). The third is contemplation of a corpse in various stages of decay with the understanding that our own body is bound to fall apart as well.

Contemplation of feeling tones, which requires recognizing the three hedonic tones of pleasant, unpleasant, and neutral, is clearly an instruction that came into existence at an early stage in the transmission of the texts. The same holds for contemplation of different states of mind, such as recognition of lust, anger, and delusion being either present or absent in the mind, or else noting whether the mind is concentrated or not concentrated, etc. The fourth establishment of mindfulness has as its early core the contemplation of the seven awakening factors: mindfulness, investigation-of-states, energy, joy, tranquillity, concentration, and equipoise. These seven qualities quite literally awaken the mind to its true potential.

A comparative survey of the four establishments of mindfulness also shows that most of these practices come with an emphasis on the present moment (Anālayo 2019d). Such an emphasis is already evident in early Buddhism and is not a subsequent innovation.

In addition to the detailed survey found in the Discourse on the Establishments of Mindfulness, there is also a collection of shorter discourses on this topic. The discourses in this collection repeatedly present a basic formula for the four establishments of mindfulness (see Anālayo 2020d: 100f), found also in the Discourse on the Establishments of Mindfulness (Anālayo 2013: 254). For the first establishment of mindfulness, contemplation of the body, the Pāli version of this basic formula proceeds in this way:

> In regard to the body one abides contemplating the body, diligent,
> clearly knowing, and mindful, free from greedy desires and
> discontent in the world.

The same formula applies to feeling tones, states of mind, and
dharmas. Regarding the last of these, the term "dharma" can
have a range of different meanings in the discourses (Anālayo
2003b: 182–186). Prominent among these is the Dharma as
the "teaching" of the Buddha; another prominent nuance is
that of dharma as a "state". Taken in conjunction, the fourth
establishment of mindfulness could perhaps best be understood
to require the application of specific "teachings" to our present
mental "state".

In sum, in relation to body, feeling tones, states of mind, and
dharmas, mindfulness occurs in collaboration with diligence and
clear knowing, leading to freedom from desires and discontent.

MONITORING WITH MINDFULNESS

The respective domain of practice is repeated for each of the
four establishments of mindfulness. In the above passage on
the first establishment, this takes the form of contemplating the
body "in regard to the body". This repetition of the domain of
practice appears to imply contemplating a particular dimension
of the body out of the general phenomenon of the body, a
sub-body, so to speak, out of the overall body (Anālayo 2003b:
33). The same then holds for the other three establishments of
mindfulness.

This instruction seems to reflect a monitoring quality of
mindfulness, in the sense of the ability to have a comprehensive
vision of a situation and thereby apperceive relationships
between its various aspects. An application of this monitoring
quality of mindfulness was already evident with the steps of
mindfulness of breathing, surveyed in the last chapter, where
the meditative task was to be aware of a range of different
aspects alongside continuous mindfulness of the process of
breathing. In the present case, a particular dimension of our own

body can be contemplated as reflecting the general nature of bodies. The same then applies to the other three establishments of mindfulness.

The nuance of a broad vision cultivated through mindfulness that aids in interrelating various aspects also becomes evident in another qualification in the instructions. According to this qualification, mindfulness should be cultivated internally, externally, and then both together as internally-and-externally. This incorporation of the internal and the external dimensions, already discussed above in Chapter 2 (see p. 20), neatly illustrates the potential of mindfulness to lead to a comprehensive view of what is taking place.

DILIGENCE IN SUPPORT OF MINDFULNESS

The basic formula translated above relates mindfulness to two other qualities, which are diligence and clear knowing. The quality of diligence reflects the need to dedicate ourselves to the practice. The basic implication appears to be the need for a balanced but sustained application of energy or effort to the practice (Anālayo 2003b: 34–39).

The explicit mention of a need to sustain mindfulness in this way is significant in view of a trend in some later Buddhist traditions to emphasize mindfulness practice primarily in the form of resting in a condition naturally inherent in the mind, a topic to which I will return in a later chapter. Already in early Buddhism, mindfulness relates to a considerable degree of non-interference and receptive observation (Anālayo 2019f). In fact, in the Discourse on the Establishments of Mindfulness the various exercises to be cultivated do not refer to mindfulness itself, but rather indicate that the practitioner contemplates, examines, compares, and knows (Anālayo 2013: 36f). These activities take place in the presence of mindfulness, which itself is less something to be done and more something "to be".

In the context of *satipaṭṭhāna* meditation, mindfulness is paired with a diligent, even ardent, application of energy and effort to the practice. This is not required for all modalities of mindfulness, in fact in the next chapter I will take up a form of practice where the passive and receptive qualities of mindfulness stand out more strongly. However, for the four establishments of mindfulness to lead to awakening, diligence clearly has its place. Gunaratana (1991/1992: 164) explains:

> Mindfulness cannot be cultivated by struggle. It grows by realizing, by letting go, by just settling down in the moment and letting yourself get comfortable with whatever you are experiencing. This does not mean that mindfulness happens all by itself. Far from it. Energy is required. Effort is required. But this effort is different from force. Mindfulness is cultivated by a gentle effort.

CLEAR KNOWING

Out of the various meditative activities mentioned in the Discourse on the Establishments of Mindfulness, perhaps the most frequent reference is to what the practitioner "knows". The verb employed here relates etymologically to "clear knowing" referenced in the basic formula. Alongside diligence, this is another key quality that serves in support of mindfulness.

In the instructions in the Discourse on the Establishments of Mindfulness, what is to be known is frequently presented in the form of direct speech, giving the impression that some degree of conceptual knowing is required. When experiencing a painful feeling tone, for example, we should know "I feel a painful feeling tone." This shows that, at least in early Buddhist thought and meditation practice, mindfulness can coexist with concepts. It not only can coexist with them, but the judicious use of concepts even makes an important contribution when cultivating the four establishments of mindfulness for the purpose of liberation (Anālayo 2003b: 40–42 and 113, 2017c: 21f, and 2018i: 7–9). I will return to the role of concepts in the next chapter.

The quality of clear knowing in combination with mindfulness appears to be the central factor in the arising of meditative wisdom. Grounded in the balanced and comprehensive vision of phenomena that becomes possible through mindfulness, the deployment of clear knowing can arouse and ripen liberating insight.

The need for a collaboration of these two distinct qualities has in some later Buddhist traditions led to a fusion of the two. Similar to the association of a more focused form of attention with mindfulness in general and with mindfulness of breathing in particular, as discussed in the previous chapter, some degree of blending of mindfulness with clear knowing appears to have happened. As a result, mindfulness has become conceptualized as a quality intrinsically conjoined with wisdom and discrimination.

This perspective is perhaps a natural development in view of the potential of mindfulness for the arousing of wisdom. Yet, it runs the risk of obfuscating to some extent the actual contribution made by mindfulness to the development of wisdom. In the early discourses, mindfulness is not invariably a quality that involves wisdom (Anālayo 2018h). This is particularly evident in the recurrent references to wrong forms of mindfulness, already mentioned in a previous chapter (see above p. 34). An instance of wrong mindfulness could hardly be an expression of wisdom.

Another relevant indication can be found in a simile that involves giving medical treatment to a person who has been shot by a poisoned arrow (Anālayo 2011: 611). Here mindfulness corresponds to the probe used by the physician to determine the exact location of the arrow, whereas wisdom has its counterpart in the surgeon's knife employed to cut open the wound such that the arrow can be extracted. The two tools are clearly complementary, yet at the same time each fulfils a distinct function.

Yet another simile surveys the various parts of an elephant's body (see Anālayo 2020d: 206). Whereas mindfulness corresponds to the neck, wisdom is the head of the elephant. As in the case of the probe and the knife, the neck and the head of the elephant are distinct, though closely related to each other.

In the same way, in early Buddhist thought mindfulness and wisdom are distinct qualities, though closely related to each other (see also below p. 115).

BALANCE

The basic formula, translated above, also refers to being "free from greedy desires and discontent in the world". This sets the direction for a cultivation of the establishments of mindfulness, which are precisely meant to lead to such freedom. At first, this freedom will be temporary and provisional, but eventually it will become final and definite. The Discourse on the Establishments of Mindfulness concludes by mentioning various time periods within which the two highest levels of awakening, recognized in early Buddhism, can be reached (Anālayo 2003b: 250–252). At these levels of awakening, sensual desire and anger have been entirely eradicated from the mind and do not stand a chance of manifesting again.

Long before such complete eradication has been accomplished, the basic potential of staying aloof from reacting with desire and aversion, even for a short moment, is an important dimension of mindfulness practice in early Buddhism. This quality could be related to a frequent qualification of mindfulness in its current clinical application as "non-judgmental" (Anālayo 2019a: 12). Such a qualification is best understood in a way that does not preclude the possibility of any evaluation. As already mentioned in Chapter 4 on embodied mindfulness, contemplation of the anatomical parts of the body, for example, requires an element of evaluation.

The notion of being non-judgmental would therefore work best if understood as pointing to the absence of reactivity by way of desire or aversion. This is indeed a central feature of mindfulness, which fosters a receptive attitude towards what happens such that we are fully aware of it but do not immediately and impulsively react to it. In the words of Gunaratana (1991/1992: 151):

> Mindfulness is non-judgmental observation. It is that ability of the mind to observe without criticism. With this ability, one sees things without condemnation or judgment ... the meditator observes experiences very much like a scientist observing an object under a microscope ... to see the object exactly as it is.

This non-reactive dimension of mindfulness has considerable potential, as it helps to free us from habitual patterns of automatic reactivity and forestalls hasty decisions and impulsive reactions that we will later regret.

SUMMARY

The basic formula of the establishments of mindfulness seems to reflect a monitoring function of mindfulness, evident in the instruction to contemplate a particular aspect of the body (and of feeling tones, states of mind, and dharmas) out of the general phenomena of the body (and feeling tones, states of mind, and dharmas).

Such contemplation comes with a clear emphasis on being in the present moment and involves mindfulness in collaboration with the qualities of diligence and clear knowing. Although closely related to mindfulness, clear knowing is a distinct mental quality and not an intrinsic property of mindfulness itself. It is only in later times that mindfulness comes to be seen as inherently involving discrimination and wisdom. The actual collaboration of mindfulness with clear knowing involves the judicious use of concepts. This differs from some later practice traditions, where the absence of concepts is seen as mandatory for successful mindfulness meditation.

The basic formula also refers to the absence of greedy desires and discontent, thereby reflecting a balanced and non-reactive attitude as an important dimension of mindfulness. Staying free of reactivity, which can be related to the notion of "non-judgmental" mindfulness, reveals a protective dimension of mindfulness that helps prevent impulsive actions.

PRACTICE SUGGESTIONS

In order to put into practice the four establishments of mindfulness, the breath can continue to serve as our main object of meditation. Based on the mode of practice described in the previous chapter, we could try to discern each of the four domains of the establishments of mindfulness in the experience of mindful breathing:

The breath takes place in the *body* and because of motions of the *body*, which can be kept in embodied awareness alongside the breath. The experience of the breath is based on *feeling* the air flowing in and out, which serves to distinguish inhalations from exhalations. The actual noting of the breath requires making mindfulness predominant in the *mind*, which is where body, feeling tone, breath, etc. are known. In this way, being mindful of the breath can be understood to involve these three dimensions. Directing awareness to recognizing them adds meditative depth to our cultivation of mindfulness of breathing.

The fourth establishment of mindfulness concerns dharmas. Here central aspects of the Buddha's teachings can be applied to the experience of the present moment. A key aspect of liberating insight in early Buddhism is insight into impermanence. This key aspect is quite evident in the experience of the breath, where an inhalation starts, lasts for a little while as a constantly changing flow, and then completely ends. The same pattern applies to the ensuing exhalation. Hence attending to the alternation between in-breaths and out-breaths can serve as a convenient way of becoming aware of impermanence. This would be a way of relating the practice to the domain of the fourth establishment of mindfulness and at the same time activating the potential of mindfulness meditation to engender liberating wisdom.

VII

BARE AWARENESS

With the present chapter I proceed to the notion of "bare awareness" as one of the modalities of mindfulness recognized in early Buddhist thought. I begin by examining instructions given to a non-Buddhist practitioner by the name of Bāhiya and then turn to another occasion in which a Buddhist monastic receives the same instructions. Next I examine the construction of experience and the role of concepts. In the final part of this chapter I take up the protective function of mindfulness.

THE INSTRUCTION TO BAHIYA

The Buddha's encounter with Bāhiya is reported in a Pāli discourse for which no parallel is known. This somewhat limits its relevance for an appreciation of early Buddhist perspectives on mindfulness, for which it is preferable to rely on material found not only in the Pāli tradition, but also in parallel versions. Fortunately, however, the same instruction is also found in a discourse addressed to a Buddhist monastic, in which case several parallels exist (see Anālayo 2018a, 2019h, and 2020d: 192–196). In what follows, I first take up the case of Bāhiya and then turn to this other occurrence.

The relevant Pāli discourse reports that a non-Buddhist practitioner by the name of Bāhiya, who was living far away from the whereabouts of the Buddha, had mistakenly thought himself to be already a fully awakened one. On finding out that this was not the case, he immediately took off and wandered across half of the Indian subcontinent in order to meet the Buddha, whom he expected to be able to teach him how to reach awakening.

On arrival at the monastery where the Buddha was staying, he found that the one whom he hoped to meet had gone into town on his daily alms round. Spurred on by his keen sense of urgency, Bāhiya decided to follow the Buddha into town rather than await his return. Upon meeting the Buddha on a street, Bāhiya requested to be given a teaching on the spot. After some hesitation, as the daily alms round is not quite an appropriate setting for giving teachings on how to reach awakening, the Buddha agreed and delivered a pithy instruction.

Soon after that Bāhiya was killed in an accident. The Buddha is on record for stating that Bāhiya passed away as one who had reached full awakening. This implies that the pithy instruction given by the Buddha had been sufficient to enable Bāhiya, who up to that point had not been acquainted with the Buddha's teachings, to gain full awakening on the spot. It invests this instruction with a rather remarkable potential. In the case of Bāhiya, the instruction must have been building on whatever training in morality and concentration he had already developed prior to his encounter with the Buddha.

The actual instruction begins by enjoining Bāhiya to train himself in such a way that "in what is seen there will be just what is seen". In other words, with any visual experience he should simply stay with what is actually seen. This relates back to the topic of sense restraint, already broached in Chapter 4 (see above p. 42). The instruction then continues by applying the same to hearing, sensing, and cognizing. Here the reference to sensing appears to function as an umbrella term for the experience of smell, taste, and touch. Cognizing in turn stands for what is experienced in the mind that is not the immediate result of something perceived through one of the five physical senses.

Having outlined this training in staying with unembellished sense experience, without reacting to it or proliferating it in various ways, the instruction continues in the following manner:

> Bāhiya, when for you in what is seen there will be just what is seen, in what is heard there will be just what is heard, in what is sensed there will be just what is sensed, in what is cognized there will be just what is cognized, then, Bāhiya, you will not be 'thereby'. Bāhiya, when you will not be 'thereby', then, Bāhiya, you will not be 'therein'. Bāhiya, when you will not be 'therein', then, Bāhiya, you will be neither here, nor beyond, nor between the two. This itself is the end of *dukkha*.

The cryptic references to "thereby" and "therein" require some interpretation. The first appears to imply that we are not carried away "thereby" if we are able to remain with bare awareness of what has appeared at any sense-door. This seems to involve a sidestepping of reactivity. When we successfully sidestep reactivity to what is experienced, we are not caught "therein", in the sense of appropriating what is experienced, approaching it with an attitude of self-centredness, and taking a stance on it through personal views.

With this much achieved, we no longer cling to the subject, the "here", to the object, the "beyond", or to what takes place "between the two", the act of seeing, hearing, sensing, or cognizing. All of this, taken together, then converges on stepping out of, and eventually making a definite end of, *dukkha* (a term that here stands for the predicaments of an unliberated mind). The final goal of the early Buddhist path of practice is precisely freedom from *dukkha*, from all that is "unsatisfactory".

THE SAME INSTRUCTION AGAIN

An occurrence of the same instruction in another Pāli discourse, which has several parallels, is addressed to a Buddhist monastic who features in some other discourses as someone given to pointless speculation. He is the one to whom the famous simile of the poisoned arrow is addressed, according to which someone struck by a poisoned arrow should allow the arrow to be extracted swiftly and not insist on first being informed about various irrelevant details regarding the archer who shot him, the nature of the bow employed on that occasion, etc. (Anālayo 2011: 353–355).

As occurred for Bāhiya, the teaching given to this monastic leads him to become fully awakened. A difference is that he does not achieve this on the spot, but only after a period of practice. In fact, the discourse reports the Buddha checking to see if his instructions have been well understood. Such a checking would not have been necessary with Bāhiya. In reply to the Buddha's query, this monastic gives a detailed explanation of how he has understood the implications of the instructions. The Buddha then approves of this explanation, which means that it can be relied on as an accurate commentary on the pithy teaching itself.

The detailed explanation offered by this monastic points to the role of mindfulness in training in such a way that in the seen there will be just what is seen, etc. The monastic notes that, if mindfulness is lost, reactions of clinging or craving towards what is experienced can easily arise. Such reactions tend to involve clinging to the details of experience that can lead to the arising of unwholesome mental states. This relates to the practice of sense restraint, discussed in Chapter 4 (see above p. 42). Once we are mindful and do not grasp at such details, however, craving and clinging no longer have the same scope to manifest.

This reflects an intriguing dimension in the understanding of mindfulness in early Buddhism and shows the potential of "bare awareness". Remaining mindfully aware of whatever happens, without reacting to it, is liberating in itself. In the case of Bāhiya, it was so liberating that it enabled a non-Buddhist to become a fully awakened one on the spot.

THE CONSTRUCTION OF EXPERIENCE

The liberating potential of mindfulness in this respect can be related to the way we usually tend to construct our own experience (Anālayo 2019h). This has been studied in cognitive psychology in terms of a tendency for "perceptual prediction". Seeing an object, for example, is not just an act of receptively taking in visual information, but is largely the result of the constructive activity of the mind. On receiving a few bits of raw data, the mind swiftly steps in and constructs a whole picture, based on anticipating what is probably out there. From a subjective viewpoint, this construction goes unnoticed and its product appears to us as "real", in the sense of providing an accurate reflection of how things are in the outside world.

The way this constructing of experience occurs can be understood as an outcome of evolutionary selection. The faster the reaction to a potential source of danger or food, the higher the chances of survival. Hence it is only natural that a predictive tendency of the mind has evolved, in order to make sense quickly of the very first bits of information that have become available.

Since this type of mechanism is usually unnoticed, our subjective impression is one of experiencing things "out there". Yet, the contribution made by the mind to what appears to be out there is rather substantial. In a way, we live in a world of our own construction, and this construction is in large part based on our expectations and personal biases. These appear to us as if they were an integral part of what is out there, rather than being merely the result of our own subjective projections.

Here the cultivation of mindfulness offers a potential for deconstructing the way we tend to fabricate our own experience. This does not take the form of active interference, but rather involves a stepping back from being carried away. Any active interference would set off the constructing tendency of the mind and therefore run counter to the deconstruction required.

In terms of the instruction to Bāhiya, the task is first of all no longer being "thereby". Once we are not carried away "thereby", we no longer take such a strong stance on what is taking place and are no longer so firmly established "therein". The simple act of mindful observation can keep peeling off layer after layer of our construction of experience. The more we realize that what we perceive to be out there actually originates to a considerable degree from what is in here, the less we tend to react strongly to it. The less we react, the less we will take a firm and fixed stance on what is taking place.

THE ROLE OF CONCEPTS

The liberating role of mindfulness practice undertaken in this way does not require completely avoiding the use of concepts. The instruction to train ourselves in such a way that in what is seen there will be just what is seen involves a "bare" form of awareness. Such bare awareness fosters a simple form of experiencing that is stripped of reactivity and any embellishment of the sense data with various associations and judgements. However, it need not be considered bare to the extent of being completely non-conceptual.

Here the same applies as with sense restraint, discussed earlier. When the Buddha was walking on his alms round, he needed the help of perceptual details. Otherwise he would not have been able to recognize that in front of him there was the practitioner Bāhiya who was requesting instructions from him. For the Buddha or any other monastic to cultivate sense restraint on their alms round does not require the complete avoidance of any noting of perceptual details. Instead, it only requires not clinging to them. This takes place by remaining established in mindfulness.

According to the early Buddhist analysis of perceptual experience, seeing, hearing, and sensing things in the world involves a minimal employment of concepts. This position emerges from an aspect of the doctrine of dependent arising, which presents consciousness as standing in a reciprocal conditioning relationship with what is called "name-and-form" (Anālayo 2018g: 9–11). Here "name" stands for various mental activities that together lead to the arising of a name, in the sense of a concept that enables recognition. "Form" in turn is the experience of materiality. These two in combination impinge on consciousness.

This analysis of experience has several significant ramifications. One of these is that early Buddhist thought is not based on a mind–body dualism. Instead, consciousness as the process of being conscious of experience is placed on one side and mental activity together with experienced materiality on the other. Moreover, it implies that being conscious of a material object invariably involves the collaboration of "name" and thus, at least to a minimal degree, the input of concepts. This does not have to take the form of discursive mental chatter. But even a brief moment of seeing requires "name" and thereby the constructing of visual experience through those mental activities that are responsible for the formation of concepts.

This mode of presentation complements a topic already taken up in the last chapter, in that concepts need not be problematized in the cultivation of mindfulness. Mindfulness is indeed a quality whose cultivation can lead to increasing degrees of inner silence and a diminishing of mental chatter, rumination, and conceptual proliferation. But it can also coexist with thought activity. It is precisely such coexistence that can be so revealing, as it enables us to notice how much we are influenced by our own biases and predispositions. The exposure of our own subjective projections onto the construction of experience is a key aspect of the liberating potential of bare awareness.

MINDFULNESS AS A PROTECTION

The potential of just remaining receptively aware of any experience can be related to a protective dimension inherent in mindfulness, which becomes prominent in several similes. In addition to those already taken up in the chapter on embodied mindfulness (see above p. 40), another simile involves a gatekeeper tasked with protecting a border town. The gatekeeper needs to be wise enough to be able to recognize and prevent enemies from getting inside (see Anālayo 2020d: 36–38). The role played by the gatekeeper in this simile illustrates the protection afforded through mindfulness in collaboration with discernment.

Yet another simile describes two acrobats who are to perform together (see Anālayo 2020d: 116–119). For both to perform well, each needs to ensure their own protection first. Having established such self-protection, each will then be able to take care of the other. As the explanation of the simile in the relevant discourse clarifies, such self-protection relies on the cultivation of the establishments of mindfulness. Based on self-protection, the two acrobats are able to perform their feats and gain their livelihood without risking an accident. The simile makes the explicit point that concern for the other should not take precedence over the need to establish ourselves first of all in the necessary inner balance. The same applies more generally to any other livelihood or undertaking, in that the foundation laid through cultivating mindfulness is essential. Doing what is needed to build up that foundation will go a long way towards ensuring that unnecessary accidents are avoided and that the required actions, be these simple work tasks or acrobatic feats, are well performed.

SUMMARY

The pithy instructions given to Bāhiya, which enabled his instant and full awakening despite being previously unacquainted with Buddhist doctrine, exemplify the potential of "bare awareness". By remaining mindful of what is seen, heard, sensed, and cognized as it is, it becomes possible to sidestep the innate tendency to be carried away by experience and take a strong stance on it through clinging. This opens up the possibility of becoming aware of the very construction of experience and the impact of our own expectations and preferences on what we perceive. Such bare awareness does not require completely dismantling the use of concepts. It only requires establishing a non-judgemental attitude, in the sense of not allowing subjective bias to have free rein by way of craving and clinging.

PRACTICE SUGGESTIONS

In the approach to mindfulness of breathing described in the previous chapter, cultivating the relationship between mindfulness and wisdom took the form of attending to the impermanent nature of the breath. Based on familiarity with impermanence, evidenced in each moment of an inhalation and an exhalation, a further step could now be taken by being mindful of impermanence in relation to anything that might manifest during our sitting meditation. These could be sounds, or bodily sensations, or anything else. With mindfulness established on the body in the sitting posture, and with the process of breathing as an integral dimension of the experience of the whole body, we simply become aware of anything that manifests, experiencing it as a process, as something changing. Sound arises, might continue a little while as a changing process, and passes away. Sensations arise, might continue a little while as a changing process, and pass away.

We gradually learn to open up to experience in the present moment in whatever way it unfolds, without interfering with it, without making it into something. We no longer feel a pressing need to proliferate and immediately evaluate whatever is taking place. Instead, as much as possible we stay with the heard in what is heard and the sensed in what is sensed. By not neglecting the potential of wisdom, discussed in the last chapter, we conjoin this mode of bare and open awareness with the potential of insight into impermanence. This need not require mental verbalization, but can simply be a silent knowing of things as a process, an opening up to the flux of experience and its inherent fluidity.

VIII

MINDFULNESS AND HEALTH

In this chapter I continue with a topic already broached in the first chapter in relation to instructions on mindful eating, namely the relationship of the cultivation of mindfulness to health. I begin with instructions given to a lay disciple on how to deal with the pains of old age. This leads me to the topic of mindfully facing pain, which shares similarities with the practice of bare awareness, explored in the last chapter, in so far as it involves being with the actual experience instead of getting caught in reactivity.

The problem of pain serves as a convenient entry point for further pursuing the early Buddhist doctrine of dependent arising, a topic also broached in the previous chapter. Another central teaching in early Buddhism concerns seven "factors of awakening", the first of which is mindfulness. This teaching relates to the theme of the present chapter, as the discourses report instances of physical healing occurring on hearing these seven awakening factors being recited, a recitation that can safely be assumed to have inspired a concurrent meditative cultivation.

ADVICE TO AN AGEING LAY DISCIPLE

Comparable to the instructions on mindful eating given to King Pasenadi for countering his tendency to overeat, discussed in Chapter 1 (see above p. 8), another discourse reports the Buddha offering practical advice to an ageing lay disciple (Anālayo 2016b: 17–26). The lay follower had approached the Buddha and described his aged condition and unstable health. In the Pāli version of this discourse, the advice he received from the Buddha took the form of the following instruction:

> You should train yourself in this way: 'my body being afflicted, my mind will not be afflicted!'

Inspired by this succinct instruction, the lay disciple approached a monastic and received an explanation of this injunction. The gist of this exposition seems to concern the problem of clinging. To the degree to which there is either clinging to the body with a sense of self-importance or else an appropriation of the body with a strong sense of ownership (and the concomitant assumption of being entitled to the body being always healthy and functioning well), to that degree any affliction of the body will inevitably become more distressful.

As long as the body serves as a source of pleasure, it is only natural that we cling and attach. Yet, the more we cling and attach at such times, the more we will suffer when the body turns into a source of pain. Conversely, if we cling less at times of pleasure, we will suffer less at times of pain. In other words, the way out of this dilemma is to learn to experience both pleasure and pain without clinging and attachment. This, however, is easier said than done. It requires a gradual training.

Mindfulness can be a central tool here, particularly in its deconstructing aspect, discussed in the last chapter. Once it has become clear that the situation in which we find ourselves is to a considerable degree the product of our own mental construction, this opens the door to changing the situation. Instead of just expecting outer conditions to change so that we are at ease, we can learn to adjust inwardly to whatever conditions present themselves. In the case of bodily affliction, in principle it is possible to experience physical pain without mental affliction. However much bodily pain and its mental repercussions may seem, from the subjective viewpoint, to be inextricably interwoven, closer inspection with mindfulness shows that this is not the case. Physical pain does not have to afflict the mind.

Needless to say, both bodily pain and mental affliction due to reacting to pain are experienced in the mind. The distinction drawn here concerns the source of feeling tones. Are these triggered by the condition of the body, or are they the result of mentally reacting to the body's condition? The latter can be avoided and this is the central point the Buddha made in his advice to the ageing lay disciple. The same principle is the theme of the simile of the arrow, to which I turn next.

THE ARROW OF PAIN

The instructions that lead up to the simile of the arrow begin by distinguishing the way the experience of feeling tones impacts two types of person (Anālayo 2016b: 27–34). One of these two types is someone untrained in the teachings, which here would refer in particular to someone who has not trained in mindfulness. The other person is someone who is trained.

Both types of person experience bodily pain, but their reactions differ substantially. The untrained person reacts with crying and wailing; the trained person does not cry and wail. The different reactions of the two have further repercussions. The untrained person has aversion to the experience of pain and, not knowing any other alternative, craves for sensual enjoyment as a way of escaping from the pain. In this way, the cycle of craving and attachment continues to be reinforced. In contrast, the trained person does not have aversion to pain. For this reason, the mind is much less afflicted by the bodily pain. Due to the mental balance established in this way, there is also no pressing need to find some sensual enjoyment as a way of escaping from the pain. In this way, inner balance and freedom from attachment continue to become stronger.

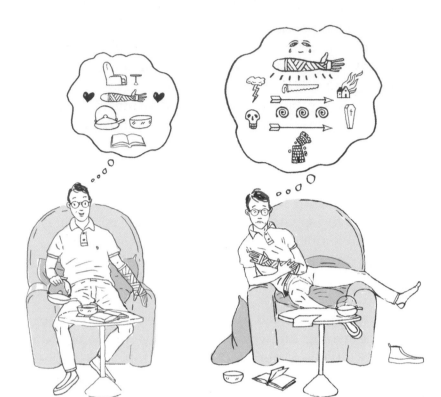

The description offered in this discourse reveals the broader repercussions of the basic predicament of pain. The underlying principle of these repercussions then finds illustration in a simile that involves being shot by an arrow. This imagery would have been inspired by ancient Indian warfare, in which being shot by an arrow must have been a regular occurrence.

In this simile, bodily pain is one arrow, and mental pains are an additional arrow. The untrained person is like someone who, after being shot by one arrow, gets shot by another. Although the discourse does not state this explicitly, I imagine a battle situation where a warrior is shot by one arrow. Because of being afflicted by the pain, he reacts in an unwise manner that exposes him to the enemy forces, who seize the opportunity to shoot him again. As a result, he gets hit by yet another arrow. In contrast, the trained person only gets hit by a single arrow. In line with the suggested interpretation, here the second warrior is careful to avoid reacting to the pain in a way that exposes him and enables the enemy forces to shoot him again. In terms of the advice given to the ageing lay disciple, the second warrior's mind did not become afflicted when the body was afflicted.

CONTEMPLATION OF FEELING TONES

How to avoid being shot by additional arrows? How to keep the mind unafflicted when the body is afflicted? The answer to such questions is found in the cultivation of mindfulness, in particular of the second establishment of mindfulness (Anālayo 2003b: 156–172, 2013: 117–141, and 2018i: 103–125). The basic instruction for the second establishment of mindfulness requires recognizing clearly what type of feeling tone is present. In the case of painful (or at least unpleasant) feeling tones, this proceeds as follows:

> When feeling a painful feeling, one knows: 'I feel a painful feeling.'

All that is required is just a simple act of clear recognition. By dint of this very act of recognition, it becomes possible to avoid being victimized by feeling. Moreover, mindfully staying with the actual experience of pain as such prevents us getting lost in associations, reactions, and conceptual proliferations in relation to the pain. These additional arrows can at times be more afflictive than the physical pain itself.

In addition to this potential of remaining mindful of the bare experience of pain, there is also a contribution to be made by insight. This involves an understanding already touched on in the practice instructions in the last two chapters: attending to impermanence.

Applying this insight to the experience of pain and death is the theme of a discourse that records the Buddha paying a visit to monastics in the sick ward (see Anālayo 2013: 134 and 2020d: 153). The instructions given on this occasion highlight the importance of understanding that feeling tones are impermanent phenomena. Feeling tones arise in dependence on the existence of the body. The body is clearly impermanent, so how could the feeling tone experienced at present, however strongly it may manifest, be permanent? Such understanding supports mindfulness in its task of decoupling mental reactions from the physical experience of pain. In fact, it can even help us face death with mental balance.

DEPENDENT ARISING

The ability to prevent bodily affliction from spilling over into the mind can be approached with the help of a central teaching in early Buddhist thought, namely the doctrine of dependent arising. The basic concern of this doctrine is to show that *dukkha* arises due to specific conditions. Discerning these conditions enables us to adjust in such a way that the influence of these conditions is diminished and eventually overcome for good. The standard exposition of this doctrine involves a series of different links that lead up to *dukkha*. Two such links came up in the last chapter: consciousness and name-and-form. For my present purposes, however, of special interest are another two links: feeling tone and craving.

Feeling tone, as the affective quality of experience, serves as a condition for craving. Feeling tone as a given of our experience is a condition that, within the scope of a normal human life, cannot be avoided. In the case of pain, this is the first arrow. Even a fully awakened one is subject to this arrow. The reaction to feeling tone by way of craving, however, is not a given of experience. Feeling tone need not result in craving. The experience of pain need not lead to craving for the pain to go away or to craving for sensual indulgence as an escape from pain. The same experience of pain can simply be met with mindfulness. When pain is met with mindfulness, the dependent arising of *dukkha* can be intercepted at the stage of feeling tone, which would otherwise serve as a condition for the arising of craving.

The potential of interrupting the dependent arising of *dukkha* at this particular juncture of dependent arising would explain why feeling tones have become the object of an entire establishment of mindfulness (Anālayo 2018j: 47–50). It is hardly surprising that body and mind have been chosen for the systematic cultivation of mindfulness, which are the first and third establishments of mindfulness (I turn to the fourth below). With the mind already covered, it is remarkable that an aspect of the mind, feeling, is singled out as the theme of the second establishment of mindfulness. The rationale behind this may well be the immense liberating potential of cultivating mindfulness in relation to feeling tones.

THE AWAKENING FACTORS

A prominent concern of the fourth establishment of mindfulness appears to echo a recurrent contrast made in the discourses between two sets of opposing mental states (Anālayo 2013: 174–176). One of these sets covers the "hindrances", five mental conditions that quite literally *hinder* the proper functioning of the mind. These are:

- sensual lust,
- anger,
- sloth-and-torpor,
- restlessness-and-worry,
- doubt.

The second set covers the seven "awakening factors", which stand in direct contrast to the five hindrances. They are:

- mindfulness,
- investigation-of-states,
- energy,
- joy,
- tranquillity,
- concentration,
- equipoise.

These seven mental qualities can *awaken* the mind's true potential. First and foremost, they do so by leading to liberation.

But they can also enable us to make the most of our mind's abilities and potential well before the attainment of liberation. The awakening factors can enliven the mind and make it be more awake to the present moment.

The foundational mental quality among these seven awakening factors, mentioned first in the standard listing, is mindfulness. The other six awakening factors fall into two groups. Three factors arouse the mind and energize it: investigation-of-states, energy, and joy. The other three factors calm the mind and settle it: tranquillity, concentration, and equipoise.

These two groups of three should be cultivated according to what circumstances demand. If the mind is sluggish, the energizers are commendable; if it is agitated, the calmers are appropriate. But at all times, mindfulness is required. Mindfulness is the one foundational quality that all the others rely on and relate to. In short, mindfulness is always useful.

The teaching on the awakening factors is relevant to the overall topic of this chapter, as the discourses report that a recitation of these seven mental qualities led accomplished monastics and the Buddha to recover from physical illness (Anālayo 2013: 212–215, 2016b: 43–50, and 2017d). The recital can safely be assumed to have inspired a concurrent meditative cultivation of these seven qualities in the mind. It must have been due to the resultant mental condition and its effect on the body that the disease was overcome.

As a side note, this concords with a point made in the last chapter, in that the cultivation of mindfulness, or even of all awakening factors, does not invariably require leaving behind all concepts. In the present case this is obvious, as the remarkable effect described in these texts took place based on hearing a recitation.

Reports of this remarkable effect on the Buddha himself offer the additional indication that it was on re-experiencing the taste of awakening that his disease vanished (see Anālayo 2020d: 157). On this understanding, the recitation would have led to a meditative arousal of those very awakening factors in the mind that were also present when the Buddha attained awakening. The resonance created in the mind with that extraordinary occasion when he became a Buddha would consequently have had such an impact on his overall bodily condition that the disease was overcome. Presumably recollecting his earlier having overcome all mental disease, through realizing awakening, was now able to effect an alleviation of even physical disease.

Here the early Buddhist conception of supreme mental health, gained through awakening, converges with bodily health as understood in medicine. This to some extent mirrors the employment of an ancient Indian medical scheme of diagnosis to formulate the key doctrine of early Buddhism in the form of the four noble truths (see above pp. 13 and 21).

SUMMARY

A central aspect of the early Buddhist recommendations for how to face old age and disease is to avoid the mind becoming afflicted when the body is afflicted. Applied to the case of pain, this advice can be illustrated with the help of a simile of being shot by arrows. The bodily pain is one arrow. Reacting to bodily pain with aversion and grief is comparable to being shot by an additional arrow. This additional arrow can be avoided. A central tool here is mindfulness: its potential may well explain why exploring feeling tones is one of the four establishments of mindfulness.

In the context of the doctrine of dependent arising, feeling tone is the place where reactions under the influence of craving can arise. Such reactions, however, need not arise. It is possible to face the experience of even strong feeling tones without reacting with craving and thereby without fuelling the conditioned arising of *dukkha*. This becomes possible through mindfulness.

In addition to the liberating potential of mindfulness in relation to the experience of pain, a direct impact on health emerges with the awakening factors. Mindfulness is the first of these seven mental qualities, which the discourses present as potentially serving to help overcome a disease (at least in the case of someone who has already personally experienced a level of awakening).

PRACTICE SUGGESTIONS

A central point that emerges from the present chapter is the need to learn how to face painful feeling tones with balance. The practice of sitting in meditation and being mindful of the breath can be used for this purpose. Whatever posture we might have adopted, sooner or later the body is going to give rise to unpleasant feeling tones. There could be a sense of pressure or tension somewhere or an itch that feels as if it really needs scratching right away. It might become too cold or too warm, we might be thirsty or hungry, or else we feel an urge to go to the bathroom.

Any of these occurrences can become an opportunity for mindful exploration. The task is simply to be mindful of the push in the mind towards taking some action. This requires waiting for a moment before taking the required action. Eventually, of course, we do take action. The point is not to turn meditation into some form of self-torture and sit through excruciating pain without moving. The suggestion is only to wait for a moment or two before stretching or scratching or doing whatever else is needed.

During the opportunity afforded to us by this moment of pausing before acting, we just remain mindfully observant of the way the unpleasant or painful feeling tones impact the mind. We witness how they clamour for some action to be taken, how they exert a push on us. This push can become our direct experience of the role of feeling tone as a potential condition for the arising of craving.

The moment of pausing and just watching, in turn, shows the potential of just being with pain instead of immediately reacting to it. Learning to be with pain through mindfulness in this way can eventually transform our entire relationship to pain, disease, and even death, the topic of the next chapter.

IX

MINDFULNESS AND DEATH

From the topics of old age and disease, taken up in the last chapter, I now proceed to what is perhaps the ultimate challenge of human existence: the undeniable fact that all life ends in death.

I begin my exploration with findings from cognitive psychology regarding an ingrained tendency to avoid recognizing our own mortality. Relevant research has revealed two main defensive strategies. I take up each of these in turn and relate them to relevant mindfulness exercises described in the early Buddhist discourses. The first of these is contemplation of a decaying corpse, which is part of the instructions for the first establishment of mindfulness. The second is a particular modality of turning with mindfulness to the process of breathing, which conjoins the experience of the present breath to the understanding that, in principle, this could be our last breath.

In the final part of this chapter I explore an association made in early Buddhist thought between the gaining of liberation and the realization of the deathless. This provides a convenient approach to understanding the notion of liberation, in that a fully awakened one has gone completely beyond any fear of death.

TERROR MANAGEMENT THEORY

The repercussions of the fear of death on various aspects of human behaviour have been studied in detail in contemporary psychology, leading to the development of what is at times referred to as the "Terror Management Theory", a *theory* on how we as human beings *manage* our existential *terror*. This terror arises from the conjunction of two conditions. One of these is the instinct for self-preservation, which we share with animals. The other is that we know that our attempts at self-preservation will not be ultimately successful. Soon or later, we have to die.

In order to avoid the terror that arises on recognizing our inability to ensure our enduring survival, there is an ingrained tendency to avoid acknowledging that we do have to die. This tendency operates below the surface of conscious deliberation. It ensures that, as soon as the theme of mortality is about to come within the purview of our attention, defence mechanisms are triggered to help prevent or at least diminish exposure with the help of some distraction or mental avoidance.

Should distraction not suffice, denial ensues. This can take two forms. In one form of denial, death is pushed far away into the distant future. The acknowledgement that we are indeed going to die is accompanied by the reassuring assumption that this will only happen after a very long time. At that far away time in the distant future we will come back to this issue, but not now. After all, we have more important things to do at present. No need to be too concerned about death at this time, as it is still so far away. The other form of denial pretends that somehow, in a way not further specified, we are exempt from mortality. Other human beings are indeed mortal, we can hardly deny that, but somehow, in some way, we are not really subject to the same. Death is out there, but not in here.

Research has also brought to light the degree to which the terror of our own mortality leads to various strategies of fortifying our sense of identity. Strong allegiance to a particular group or belief system serves to give us a reassuring sense of being part of something that will endure. Much of religious and political fundamentalism can be traced to displaced reactivity to the fear of death. In this way, the terror of our own mortality can have widespread repercussions in a range of different ways. For this reason, learning to face the undeniable fact that we have to die has a remarkable potential, as it can help us go beyond existential anxiety and thereby beyond what can trigger a range of unwholesome reactions. Perhaps most importantly, it can help us become prepared for death and make us be much more conscious of the potential and importance of the present moment.

The best time to learn to face death is right here and now. When else could it be? Is it wise to wait until the last moment? Would we adopt the same strategy when having to pass an exam, starting to learn only on the day of the test? Is it not considerably more meaningful to train in the art of dying when we still have time to get gradually accustomed to it?

Once it has become clear that it is indeed reasonable not to push death away into the distant future and we begin to face our own mortality here and now, a fascinating transformation can occur. What earlier appeared so terribly frightening turns out to be much less so. Once we stop running away from our own shadow and turn around to look, we find that it is just a shadow, after all. At the same time, learning to live in acknowledgement of our own mortality makes us appreciate life even more. It helps us to become so much more alive to the opportunities of the present moment, to the importance of making the best use of it instead of squandering it on meaningless activities. In this way, mindfulness of death can have a remarkable impact on our priorities and our relationships, on our whole life.

CONTEMPLATION OF A CORPSE

The early Buddhist discourses offer two mindfulness-related practices that can counter each of the two forms of denial mentioned above, where we either pretend that death does not apply to us or else push it off into the distant future. These two could be summarized as "not me" and "not now". The first of these, "not me", can be countered with a practice found in the

Discourse on the Establishments of Mindfulness in the section on contemplation of the body.

The instructions describe different stages in the decay of a corpse that has been cast aside and is lying somewhere out in the open. Apparently in the ancient Indian setting this was not as uncommon as it would be in most parts of the world today. The descriptions given in the Discourse on the Establishments of Mindfulness and its parallels portray in considerable detail what happens when a corpse is left to decay (Anālayo 2003b: 152–155, 2013: 97–116, and 2018i: 83–101):

The body becomes bloated and various animals come to feast on it. Gradually the flesh disappears and the skeleton becomes visible, until eventually there are only bones. At first these bones are still held together by the tendons, forming a skeleton, but as the tendons rot away the bones become scattered and then disintegrate.

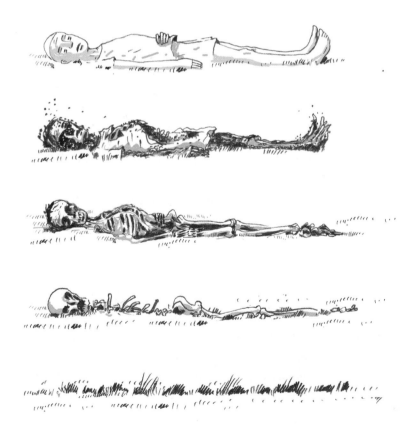

The exercise seems to involve some degree of visualization that need not necessarily be based on actually witnessing these stages, although such direct observation would of course be very supportive. With each of the various stages of decay, the Pāli version of the Discourse on the Establishments of Mindfulness recommends the following reflection, relating it to our own body:

> This body too is of the same nature; it will be like that, it is not exempt from that fate.

The main thrust of this exercise is to drive home the fact, again and again, that our own body is of the same nature as the decaying corpse. Although it need not go through exactly the same stages of decay (in modern times our body is much more likely to end up being buried or burned), the basic fact that it will eventually fall apart remains the same.

This form of mindfulness practice could easily be extended to any occasion of witnessing the mortality of others, be it humans or animals. The same reflection could be employed, either in full or else taking up a part of it that we find particularly helpful, such as the realization that our own body "is not exempt from that fate".

Practising like this will counter the form of denial of somehow pretending to ourselves that it is only others who die. The artificial barrier between ourselves and others, erected for such purposes, can in this way gradually be eroded. As a mode of mindfulness practice, this relates in particular to contemplating internally and externally, already discussed in previous chapters (see above pp. 20 and 61).

THE LAST BREATH

Besides the pretence "not me", the other strategy of denial is "not now". To counter this tendency, another exercise can be employed that also relates to mindfulness. This is based on a discourse which reports the Buddha checking how some of his disciples were cultivating mindfulness of death. When they described their practice, he found that they were still to some degree pushing death off into the future.

Pointing out that such practice was not yet a full implementation of mindfulness of death, the Buddha recommended that awareness of mortality be linked directly to the present moment. This could be done while eating, by establishing the awareness that we might die after swallowing the present morsel of food. Alternatively it could be related to breathing, in this case by establishing the similar awareness that we might die after the present breath (Anālayo 2016b: 200–207, 2018i: 90–95, and 2019j: 242f).

This approach brings mortality right into the here and now; it drastically counters the attempt to push it off into the distant future. Although it may seem somewhat radical, on reflection it becomes clear that this approach is in line with reality. We cannot be sure that life will continue beyond the present moment. Some unexpected accident might happen, some vital organ might stop working. It is indeed possible that death could be just one breath away.

This in turn makes it highly recommendable that we learn to face our own mortality right now, in order to prepare for the unknown time when we actually have to pass away. The time to undertake such preparation is none other than the present. Failing to do so, we will be unprepared when we have to breathe our last breath.

From the viewpoint of mindfulness, the present exercise highlights in particular the chief quality of being in the present moment. The sustained practice of mindfulness of death in this way will make us become ever more alive to the present moment and its potential. Our priorities become clear and we meet each moment fully, in the awareness that we are never completely sure if there will be another chance.

To some degree the present exercise also relates to the internal and external dimensions of mindfulness, in so far as those who have learnt to face their own mortality are fully able to be with others who are passing away. To the degree to which we no longer deny our own mortality, to that degree we can better help others who are confronted by death.

THE DEATHLESS

Early Buddhist thought envisions the possibility that, with sustained practice, we can completely go beyond any fear of death. One of the qualifying characteristics of a fully awakened one is precisely a total transcendence of the terror of mortality.

The attainment of awakening is regularly expressed as a realization of the "deathless". The idea of the deathless is a notion taken from the ancient Indian cultural background, but invested with a specific Buddhist meaning. Rather than being some form of immortality that avoids death and leads to eternal bliss in some heavenly realm, the deathless becomes something attainable while still alive. Having gone completely beyond the fear of death is the deathless. It is the deathless, because death has lost its sting.

Insight into the predicament of mortality and the related predicaments of old age and disease feature regularly in the discourses as what motivates the quest for awakening. These could in fact be included under the heading of death, in so far as old age can be viewed as gradual dying and disease can be considered a temporary death of the body's proper functioning. In the end it all comes down to the loss of control over "my body" and "my life".

The Buddha himself is on record for having been inspired to seek awakening after having recognized the basic human dilemma of being subject to disease, old age, and death, a topic I will take up again in the next chapter. When he first announced his awakening to others, the discourses report that he proclaimed he had realized "the deathless" (Anālayo 2016b: 117).

This notion of the deathless can help translate the early Buddhist conception of awakening into something relevant and comprehensible to those from a variety of different backgrounds. The fact of death is undeniable and allegiance to a particular religious or secular belief system does not change this in any way. The need to face death should be equally undeniable. Given this, a cultivation of the mind that can eventually lead to total freedom from the fear of death, with all its various ramifications and repercussions, should be easily intelligible and acceptable, no matter how religious or secular we consider ourselves to be.

As with the other avenues of cultivating increasing degrees of inner freedom, surveyed in previous chapters, mindfulness can serve as a primary tool here. Mindfulness of death can counter the two main modes of denial of mortality by bringing the reality of death right into the *here* (= me) and the *now*. Every step taken in this direction can enliven our lives, clarify our priorities, open our hearts to the suffering of others, diminish our clinging to a particular belief system or identity construct, and eventually lead to the realization of the deathless.

SUMMARY

Untrained human beings are prone to experience existential terror, resulting from the conflict between the instinct for self-preservation and the knowledge that ultimately this instinct will be thwarted. At a level below conscious intention and deliberation, the mind tries to fend off recognition of mortality with the help of distraction and two strategies of denial: "not me" and "not now", imagining that death does not really apply to ourselves and anyway is something that will happen only in the distant future.

Two mindfulness meditations could help to counter these strategies of denial. One of these meditations is contemplation of a corpse in decay, which is based on the idea of relating external examples of mortality to the nature of our own body. The other requires bringing the actuality of death right into the present moment with the awareness that death could happen right now. A convenient tool for doing that is the breath.

Cultivation of the recollection of death, as well as other liberating meditation practices taught in early Buddhism, can culminate in the realization of the deathless. Such realization is possible while we are still alive and has as a distinct feature the loss of any fear of death.

PRACTICE SUGGESTIONS

A practical approach for cultivating mindfulness of death could be based on combining elements from each of the two meditations discussed above, the corpse contemplation and the yoking of the breath to the awareness that this could be our last moment. For doing so, I would recommend adopting the "corpse posture" or "corpse pose". This requires lying down flat on our backs with the heels slightly spread and the arms a few inches away from the body. If we are drowsy, it can be helpful to lift up one lower arm in such a way that the hand points towards the ceiling and the elbow rests on the ground. This posture of the lower arm can be maintained for a long time without much effort. As soon as we are about to doze off, however, the upward position of the arm will be lost. The ensuing movement of the arm collapsing downwards will wake us up and thereby prevent us from falling asleep.

Lying down in the corpse posture, we can first of all become aware of the whole body. Within that field of awareness of the whole body, we can be mindful of the natural process of breathing. While being aware of the continuity of the breathing process, we bring up the thought of our own death, the recognition that eventually this body will be lying down in the same way, but being no longer alive.

The thought of our own death can be brought up either as just a brief reminder, or else it can be contemplated in some detail, according to what feels appropriate at that time. For a more detailed reflection, we might dwell on the fact that, when passing away, we have to leave everything behind. All our possessions will no longer be ours. Our responsibilities and positions in society will have to be abandoned. Our relatives and dear ones will have to continue without us.

Based on having brought up the thought of death in whatever manner seems appropriate, we become aware of the alternation between inhalations and exhalations. With every inhalation, we give emphasis to the fact that, in principle, this could be our last breath. With every exhalation, we train ourselves to relax and let go.

Correlating these two aspects of recognizing mortality and letting go to the inhalations and exhalations respectively enables us to adjust our practice as needed. When the mind tries to dismiss the fact of death, more emphasis could be given to the inhalations. This does not involve changing the inhalation in any way, as it only requires giving more emphasis to the corresponding reflection. Breathing remains natural throughout. When the truth of our own mortality becomes too agitating, more emphasis can be given to relaxing and letting go with the exhalations. Fine-tuning the practice in this way, we gradually learn to allow death to become part of our life.

X

MINDFULNESS AND THE BUDDHA'S
QUEST FOR AWAKENING

This is the first of three chapters over the course of which I attempt to present a concise history of mindfulness. I begin by briefly surveying pre-Buddhist antecedents and then examine in detail the Buddha's quest for awakening from the viewpoint of possible relationships to mindfulness. In the next chapter, Chapter 11, I try to trace the history of mindfulness from early Buddhism to modern-day insight meditation. In Chapter 12 I instead proceed from early Buddhism to non-dual forms of mindfulness-related practices as taught in Himalayan and East Asian Buddhist meditation traditions.

Before setting out on these three chapters, I would like to state openly their limitations. The early discourses do not explicitly depict in what way the Buddha's understanding of mindfulness and its potential evolved during his quest for awakening, so the present chapter is based more on suppositions than are the preceding nine chapters. In Chapters 11 and 12, my presentation involves a considerable degree of simplification. Within the context of the present book, aimed at a general readership, it is not possible to give due room to all the complexities and details involved in the relevant textual and historical developments. Therefore I can only highlight a few selected strands that in one way or another seem to have impacted the understanding of mindfulness in different Buddhist traditions. I would like to invite the reader to take what I present here merely as a preliminary sketch. In case of further interest, studying relevant publications can lead to a more in-depth appreciation of the historical developments that I am only able to touch on superficially.

ANCIENT INDIAN PRECEDENTS

"Mindfulness" has become the standard rendering of the Pāli term *sati*, which from an etymological viewpoint carries nuances related to memory. In the ancient Indian setting, its Sanskrit counterpart *smṛti* can refer to bringing to mind something from the past but also from the present (Monier-Williams 1899/1999: 1272, Gethin 1992: 36, and Klaus 1993: 85). Already in the most ancient of Indian sacred scriptures, the *Ṛgveda*, which predates the time of the Buddha by many centuries, the corresponding verbal root (*smṛ*) can convey the sense of paying attention to something in the present (Klaus 1993: 79).

This in turn implies that the memory connotation of *sati* needs to be handled with circumspection. It would be misleading to take this connotation as implying that any occurrence of the word *sati* invariably intends a recollection of something from the past. To some extent the use of the term "memory" in this context is a misnomer; a better formulation would be, for example, to speak of "keeping in mind" or even "bringing to mind" (see also below p. 107). Such terms could help to avoid the mistaken impression that *sati* must always involve some remembrance of past events. This is not the case with pre-Buddhist precedents and holds even more so for its Buddhist usages.

The Sanskrit *smṛti* also carries the sense of a body of sacred literature passed on by oral means. An examination of the ancient Indian oral transmission from the viewpoint of current research in cognitive psychology reveals that those responsible for this transmission were trained from their early childhood onwards to memorize texts without drawing inferences (Anālayo 2019b). This in turn suggests that the ancient Indian heritage of the term we now translate as "mindfulness" could have already carried nuances of receptivity without immediate reaction, be this by drawing inferences or by reacting in any other way.

IN QUEST OF AWAKENING

The evolution of mindfulness from its pre-Buddhist precedents to its role as a central quality in the early Buddhist path to awakening can be related to aspects of the future Buddha's quest for awakening (Anālayo 2020c). Although the canonical texts do not establish such relationships overtly, I will attempt to draw out what to my mind appear to be implicit pointers to precedents for the role mindfulness eventually assumed in early Buddhist meditation. It needs to be kept in mind, however, that what follows are my suggestions and not necessarily something explicitly found in the source material.

A background to the future Buddha's primary motivation to go forth from the household life to become a renunciate emerges from a passage that describes his insight into old age, disease, and death (Anālayo 2017g: 6–8). In contrast to ordinary human beings, who might just feel disgusted when they see someone become old, sick, and pass away, in the case of the future Buddha the same sight led to the realization that he was himself bound to undergo the same.

The passage does not mention mindfulness. Nevertheless, a relation could be drawn to mindfulness cultivated internally and externally. Such cultivation would have a considerable potential to lead to insight into the similarity between the predicament of others and our own condition, instead of just turning away in disgust on seeing manifestations of old age, sickness, and death.

Once he had gone forth, the Buddha-to-be dwelled in secluded places, in the knowledge that being able to do so without fear required a range of qualities. One of these qualities was mindfulness in contrast to forgetfulness (Anālayo 2016a: 17). The relevant discourse then describes how he faced any fear, which could be triggered by the sound of some wild animal, by remaining in the same bodily posture until the fear had subsided (Anālayo 2017g: 17). Even though this passage does not explicitly refer to mindfulness, it seems fair to draw such a connection, given that the discourse previously mentions mindfulness among the qualities required for living in seclusion without fear.

In the present context, this would then involve some degree of mindfulness directed to bodily postures, which is one of the exercises found among contemplations of the body in the first establishment of mindfulness (see above p. 39, Anālayo 2003b: 136–141 and 2020d: 68). In addition, it would also require some form of awareness of the present state of mind, in order to be able to recognize the presence of fear for what it is, rather than just reacting to it. This would then correspond, in principle, to the main thrust underlying the third establishment of mindfulness, contemplation of the mind.

In sum, recognizing the presence of fear in the mind and then meeting this condition by remaining seated, or standing, etc., until the fear had subsided, could be considered as precedents for the first and third establishments of mindfulness. This is not to assert that already at that point in time the Buddha-to-be was actually practising the first and third establishments of mindfulness. The point is only to suggest that his experience while dwelling in seclusion and facing fear can be considered as forming precedents for his eventual formulation of mindfulness practice in terms of these two modes of contemplation.

Besides such contemplation of a mental state of fear, another passage reports that, during his quest for awakening, the future Buddha drew a clear-cut distinction between wholesome and unwholesome states of mind (Anālayo 2017g: 28–30). Such distinction underlies the basic recognition, required when cultivating the third establishment of mindfulness, of whether the mind is with or without unwholesome qualities like lust, anger, or delusion (Anālayo 2003b: 173–178, 2013: 142–159, and 2018i: 127–133).

According to yet another discourse, the Buddha-to-be examined his own mind to counter any inclination towards sensuality (Anālayo 2017g: 25f). Such mental states of lust can become an object of mindfulness not only in the third establishment of mindfulness, but also with contemplation of the hindrances, belonging to the fourth establishment of mindfulness. The basic difference here is that, with the third establishment of mindfulness, the task is simply recognition of the actual condition of the mind. Contemplation of the hindrances proceeds further by directing mindful exploration to the conditions that led to the arising of sensual desire or anger (etc.) in the mind, as well as the conditions that can help us to emerge from them and prevent future recurrence (Anālayo 2003b: 186 and 2018i: 150–153). From this viewpoint, perhaps the idea of examining the mind to counter any inclination towards sensuality could be a precedent for mindfully observing the conditions that lead to the arising of sensual desire.

The shift towards discerning the conditions for the presence of a defilement in the mind can also be related to another dimension of the future Buddha's quest for awakening, namely his development of the ability to enter concentrative absorption. The discourse in question mentions a range of minor defilements that he needed to overcome in order to achieve and maintain deep concentration (Anālayo 2017g: 32–39). In the course of his practice, the Buddha-to-be discovered how each of these minor defilements had caused a loss of concentration, hence by overcoming them he was able to stabilize concentration again. This reflects a practical way of working with conditionality in the mind.

Before reaching awakening, the future Buddha is on record for having engaged in ascetic practices. Even when experiencing strong pain, due to possessing mindfulness he was able to prevent his mind from becoming overwhelmed by the experience of pain (Anālayo 2017g: 57). Once he realized that such ascetic practices would not lead him to the goal of his aspiration, he changed his approach. When cultivating deep states of concentration as part of this changed approach, he maintained the same balanced attitude by ensuring that his mind did not become overwhelmed by the experience of pleasure (Anālayo 2017g: 92–94). The ability to avoid becoming overwhelmed by painful or pleasant feeling tones may well explain the emphasis on being mindful of feeling tones in his later instructions, to the extent that an entire establishment of mindfulness (the second of the four) is dedicated to this topic.

Another significant factor in the future Buddha's change of approach seems to have been his recollection of an experience of deeper concentration from a time before he engaged in asceticism (Anālayo 2017g: 78–85). This memory sparked his realization that joy and happiness as such are not necessarily obstacles to awakening. As long as they are wholesome, joy and happiness can support progress to liberation. This realization could explain why joy features as one of the seven awakening factors, qualities that awaken the mind's true potential (already mentioned above p. 85). Contemplation of these awakening factors belongs to the fourth establishment of mindfulness.

Building on mindfulness as the first of these awakening factors (1), whose relevance to the Buddha's progress to awakening is quite evident from the material surveyed above, next comes investigation of states (2). This quality of enquiry needs to be sustained by energy (3). Such sustained investigation is characteristic of the future Buddha's continuous monitoring of his own progress to awakening, where he continually investigated what could lead him to the final goal of his aspiration. Besides joy (4), already mentioned, tranquillity (5) and concentration (6) are awakening factors whose importance for cultivating the mind must have become evident to the Buddha-to-be when he developed the ability to enter concentrative absorption. The last of the seven awakening factors is equanimity or equipoise (7), a quality reflected in his ability to remain free from being overwhelmed by experiences of pleasure or pain.

The teaching of the seven awakening factors is considered a unique discovery of the Buddha (see Anālayo 2020d: 221). This makes it fair to assume that his own experiences during his quest for awakening made him realize the importance and significance of these particular mental qualities.

AWAKENING GAINED

On the night of his awakening, the Buddha is on record for first of all developing recollection of his own past lives, based on having attained the deep concentration of the fourth absorption. This appears to be a natural extension of the reflection that prompted him to abandon asceticism. After looking back on his progress so far, he realized the futility of his ascetic practices and eventually remembered an experience of absorption from a still earlier time of his life. In the context of such recollecting of events ever further back in the past, recollection of his past lives would naturally fall into place.

Such ability to recollect past lives relies on the cultivation of mindfulness (see Anālayo 2020d: 14). In this way, alongside episodes that appear to stand in the background of the practice of the four establishments of mindfulness, the practice of mindful recollection also has a direct relationship to the Buddha's quest for awakening.

Recollection of his own past lives would have led the Buddha to an insight into the constructed nature of the sense of identity, which changes from one life to the next (Anālayo 2017g: 97f). The next knowledge cultivated during the night of awakening then confirms the same principle for others, thereby proceeding along the lines of a shift from the internal to the external. This knowledge takes the form of witnessing the passing away and being reborn of other living beings in accordance with the conditions created by their own former deeds (Anālayo 2017g: 105f). Such insight would have disclosed the conditionality involved in the cycle of rebirths.

The final knowledge attained during the night of awakening was insight into and removal of the influxes (*āsava*), a term that stands for the mental influences that are responsible for keeping living beings in the bondage of the cycle of rebirths. According to a detailed exposition of methods to counter these influxes, cultivating the seven awakening factors can lead to their elimination (see Anālayo 2017g: 119–123 and 2020d: 219f). In fact, all Buddhas awaken by overcoming the hindrances, dwelling in the establishments of mindfulness, and cultivating the awakening factors (see Anālayo 2020d: 231f).

At a time soon after his awakening, the Buddha is on record for devising the scheme of the four establishments of mindfulness (see Anālayo 2017g: 102f and 2020d: 86–89). This would have been based on his own experience of the remarkable potential of mindfulness, gained during his quest for and eventual attainment of awakening. In this way the quality of mindfulness, already known in the ancient Indian setting, might have gradually acquired its central position and significance in the early Buddhist path to awakening.

As a fully awakened one, the Buddha possessed continuous mindfulness (see Anālayo 2020d: 228–230). The discourses report a special modality of the establishments of mindfulness relevant to his role as a teacher. Differing from the well-known set of four such establishments, the relevant passage speaks instead of three establishments of mindfulness (see Anālayo 2020d: 232–235). These relate to three possible situations that could occur when giving a teaching: all disciples might be listening attentively to what the Buddha teaches, or else only some of them, or else none of the disciples might be listening attentively. In any of these three situations, although fully aware of their attitude, the Buddha remained equanimous and mindful.

SUMMARY

Even in the pre-Buddhist setting, the term nowadays translated as mindfulness did not just refer to memory from the past. This makes it perhaps preferable to speak of "keeping in mind" rather than "memory" in relation to mindfulness.

Aspects of the future Buddha's progress to liberation appear to point to a gradual evolution of his employment of mindfulness and his growing realization of its potential. Dimensions of practice described in the Discourse on the Establishments of Mindfulness can be related to the future Buddha's quest, such as: awareness of postures; monitoring the impact of feeling tones; recognition of the condition of the mind by distinguishing between wholesome and unwholesome states; and working with the conditionality of the mind. Of particular importance here are the awakening factors, which the discourses reckon a distinct teaching of the Buddha. Based on a removal of the hindrances, these seven awakening factors are the qualities that ripen the mind into awakening. As mentioned earlier, the first of these is mindfulness, which forms their foundation and reference point.

With awakening attained, the Buddha continued to be established in mindfulness. When facing different reactions from his audience while giving teachings, he remained inwardly balanced by relying on the non-reactive stance of mindfulness and equanimity.

PRACTICE SUGGESTIONS

A significant aspect of mindfulness that emerges from the present chapter is its relationship to memory. From a practice-related perspective, I take this to point to a characteristic of mindfulness as a keen apperception of what takes place now in such a way that, if required, it can be more easily and correctly remembered at a later time.

Applying this understanding to the practice of mindfulness could take place by cultivating a keen interest in the present moment's experience. In the case of mindfulness of breathing, this could be fostered by arousing an almost inquisitive attitude towards the breath and the distinction between inhalations and exhalations. Approaching the in itself hardly interesting process of breathing with such an attitude helps to maintain continuity of mindfulness.

Based on having built up familiarity with this dimension of mindfulness in relation to the breath, the same could then be experimented with when engaging in various other activities during daily life. For example, imagining we are to give a detailed report to a good friend about how we executed a particular activity could help to arouse this type of attitude. It can be quite revealing to see how even the most ordinary activity, earlier perceived as a boring duty to be completed as soon as possible, can be completely transformed through establishing mindfulness in combination with an element of genuine interest and enquiry.

XI

MINDFULNESS AND ABHIDHARMA

In this chapter I attempt to trace the history of mindfulness from early Buddhism to modern-day insight meditation (*vipassanā*). In order to provide a background for appreciating this development, I need to cover several doctrinal developments that took place in the Buddhist traditions. One of these is the belief that the Buddha had been omniscient. Another is a radicalization of impermanence, leading to the notion of momentariness, the idea that phenomena disappear immediately after having arisen. Another relevant development involves a synonym for mindfulness that acquired a different meaning, as a result of which mindfulness was seen as plunging into its object.

OMNISCIENCE

After the Buddha had passed away, his extraordinary nature and abilities received increasing emphasis among later generations of his disciples. One aspect of the resultant gradual apotheosis of the Buddha was the emergence of the belief that he had been omniscient (Anālayo 2014a: 117–127). The ensuing shift in the conception of the nature of the Buddha transformed one who through awakening knew the nature of it all into one who knew all; it turned one who had seen through everything into one who had seen everything.

With the passage of time and lacking a direct relationship with the supposedly omniscient teacher, there must have been a strongly felt need to substitute for the loss of his comprehensive wisdom that had enabled him to guide disciples. In order to keep open the path to awakening discovered by the Buddha, such need for substitution appears to have been a significant driving force in the emergence of Buddhist scholasticism in the form of the Abhidharma, the "higher teaching" (Anālayo 2014a). The development of the Abhidharma began with exegeses on selected early discourses and at times even became part of the discourses during their transmission. Over time, however, the Abhidharma developed into an increasingly independent enterprise, resulting in Abhidharma treatises on their own, which eventually came to supersede in importance all other texts.

A principal thrust of the Abhidharma lies in providing a comprehensive coverage of all aspects of the Buddha's teachings, a complete map, resembling as much as possible omniscient knowledge. Such a complete map serves to ensure that those who wish to embark on the path will have all the information they need and not get lost. In this way, the Abhidharma project attempts to build a complete system out of the ad hoc teachings found in the discourses. As a result, the Buddha's pragmatic concern with the existential predicament and its resolution came to be replaced to some extent by system-building. Such system-building required some degree of de-contextualization of the various teachings given by the Buddha, which were extracted from their actual setting, in order to use them as building blocks for the system. It also required streamlining terminology to ensure consistency, which at times fuelled a tendency to reify terms and eventually led to positing a particular set of concepts as ultimate realities.

Early stages of the attempt to become ever more comprehensive can already be discerned among later parts of the early discourses, which during the process of oral transmission were influenced by the growing Abhidharma exegesis. An illustrative example would be the fourth establishment of mindfulness, contemplation of dharmas. Comparative study of the Discourse on the Establishments of Mindfulness points to the cultivation of the awakening factors (based on a removal of the hindrances) as the original concern of contemplation of dharmas. The main thrust of the fourth establishment of mindfulness would thus have been a mindful monitoring of the mind in such a way that it becomes ready for the breakthrough to awakening (Anālayo 2013: 164–176).

Given that progress to awakening requires the cultivation of insight, it is not surprising that key doctrinal teachings came to be added to contemplation of dharmas at some point during the transmission of the Discourse on the Establishments of Mindfulness. One of these is the four noble truths, a diagnostic scheme taken from ancient Indian medicine to identify the root cause of the human predicament and its resolution.

These four noble truths are the theme of what tradition considers to have been the first teaching given by the Buddha, right after his awakening. Additional emphasis on these four noble truths can then be seen in the Greater Discourse on the Establishments of Mindfulness. A detailed analysis of the four noble truths, given in this discourse, is clearly a later addition (Analayo 2014a: 94–100). The rather lengthy exposition in this part of the Greater Discourse on the Establishments of Mindfulness illustrates a basic feature evident in Abhidharma texts, where with increasing attention to various details the meditative task shifts from simply being mindful of the condition of the mind to becoming aware of an increasingly larger inventory of details to satisfy doctrinal expectations.

MOMENTARINESS

Attempts in Abhidharma thought to provide a comprehensive map naturally tend to focus on a single instant in time. It is already a rather demanding task to provide a complete coverage of something at a singular moment; it would be all the more demanding to do so over an extended period of time. A single moment of time is also a central concern of the theory of momentariness, according to which things cease immediately after they have arisen. This notion involves a radicalization of the early Buddhist teaching on impermanence, according to which phenomena can endure as changing processes for some period of time situated between their arising and their ceasing (see Anālayo 2013: 105–108).

The emergence of the theory of momentariness could have resulted from a radical implementation of the early Buddhist teaching on the absence of a permanent self, leading to the belief that there cannot be anything persisting at all in constantly changing phenomena (von Rospatt 1995: 11). The evolution of such a position is not surprising, given that already at the time of the Buddha a monastic had misinterpreted the fact of continuity to imply that it is the very same consciousness that continues from one life to another (Anālayo 2011: 252). Perhaps in an attempt to forestall such misinterpretations, the fact of change came to be viewed as involving a series of substitutions. The idea was that what is old perishes, and in its stead something new manifests that is causally closely related to the old.

Mindful contemplation of cessation has a strong potential to lead to insight into the other two characteristics of *dukkha* and not-self: because what is impermanent will sooner or later end, it is incapable of yielding lasting satisfaction, it is *dukkha*. What is impermanent and *dukkha* in turn cannot be the self, which in the ancient setting by definition stood for something permanent (and blissful). Thus viewing all phenomena as passing away, ending, vanishing, and ceasing is naturally a prominent perspective in the cultivation of mindfulness aimed at liberating insight.

The same basic thrust also underlies a set of insight themes that are to be cultivated with the awakening factors. Here cessation is the theme that leads up to the culmination of insight in letting go. Although mindful contemplation with a strong emphasis on all aspects of subjective experience as being subject to cessation can be a rather powerful mode of arousing liberating insight, this is simply a step meant to issue in letting go. In other words, it is a soteriological strategy and not an ontological statement that everything ceases immediately after having appeared.

A problem resulting from the notion of momentariness is how to provide a coherent explanation of continuity. How to account for the persistence of personality traits and the ability to remember when everything ceases as soon as it has arisen? This type of question would naturally have stimulated an interest in the topic of memory and its relationship to mindfulness.

MEMORY

One of the chief modalities of the Abhidharma project of providing a comprehensive coverage of phenomena takes the form of listing synonyms for key terminology. The discourses regularly employ sets of synonyms, which in the ancient Indian oral setting served to safeguard against loss. A set of similar expressions stands much greater chance of being remembered than a single word and also better impresses itself on the audience (Anālayo 2011: 15 and 2019f). The same feature becomes a prominent Abhidharma tool, where definitions of key terms regularly attempt to provide an exhaustive listing of synonyms in an overall attempt to streamline terminology and make it more consistent, in contrast to its somewhat free and variable usage in the early discourse.

In the case of mindfulness, such listings of synonyms tend to include various terms related to its semantic nuance of memory. In search of relevant occurrences among the teachings given by the Buddha and his disciples, one Pāli discourse in particular would have attracted interest with its description of how someone reborn in a celestial realm regains memory that had been lost at the time of passing away (see Anālayo 2019f). Such a situation must have been of particular interest in view of the challenge of explaining such ability, once the mind is seen as a quick succession of momentary mental states that pass away as soon as they have arisen. In such a scenario, how could such memory, after having been lost, be retrieved again at a later time while being in a different type of body in another realm of existence?

The discourse describes that the person in question had memorized the teachings but passed away with a loss of mindfulness. The passage in question employs the verb *apilapati* to explain how this person was able to remember what had earlier been memorized, after having been reborn in a celestial realm. The term *apilapati* is somewhat obscure. Probably it refers to recovering memory when hearing others recite the same texts that this person had earlier memorized.

A reinterpretation or misunderstanding of this term in turn resulted in associating a different meaning with it, namely not floating and hence plunging into the object of the mind. Given the ambivalent sense of the expression in its original context, it is not surprising that its original meaning did not remain clear. Moreover, in order to become part of a list of synonyms, the term had to be extracted from its original setting in the discourse and thus was de-contextualized. Lacking a context, its implications can of course be more easily misunderstood.

As a result, mindfulness came to be understood as a quality that "plunges into" an object and thereby ensures the absence of mental floating (Gethin 1992: 38–40). In early Buddhist thought, mindfulness on its own appears to be more a receptive and non-interfering quality. On the above understanding, however, mindfulness becomes considerably more active and to some degree fused with focused attention (see Anālayo 2019f and 2020d: 43–45).

Another dimension of the apparently ongoing exploration of the memory nuance of mindfulness appears to have led to a comparable fusion of qualities that in early Buddhist thought are treated as distinct, namely mindfulness and wisdom. In later texts in the Pāli tradition the reasoning seems to have been that, since it is through mindfulness that one remembers, this associative function means that mindfulness enables one to see things in relation to each other (Gethin 1992: 42). Hence, in a way, mindfulness means to see things in their interrelationship and thus more accurately. For this reason, mindfulness must be intimately bound up with wisdom. In this way, eventually mindfulness came to be considered an invariably wholesome quality that is conjoined with wisdom.

In the early discourses, by contrast, mindfulness is ethically neutral. It results in wisdom when it occurs in the company of clear knowing (*sampajañña*) or else in combination with the second awakening factor of investigation of states (*dhammavicaya*). In other words, what in early Buddhism is a compound, "mindfulness and clear knowing" (*sati-sampajañña*), or a collaboration of two distinct awakening factors, in later times seems to have become intrinsic to mindfulness itself.

A correlation of the factors of the eightfold path with the three trainings in morality, concentration, and wisdom places right mindfulness in the division of concentration instead of the division of wisdom (see Anālayo 2018c: 1048 and 2020d: 204). This implies that in early Buddhist thought mindfulness was seen as a quality distinct from wisdom, otherwise this correlation would not have arisen in the first place. It confirms that the notion of mindfulness as necessarily implying discrimination and wisdom is a later development (see also above p. 63).

INSIGHT MEDITATION

The widespread practice of insight meditation in modern times harks back to Myanmar (Burma) at the time of the British colonial rule. In order to fortify lay Buddhists against the influences of foreign domination and to ensure the longevity of Buddhism, Abhidharma teachings were made accessible to laity on a wide scale (Brown 2013). According to tradition, the disappearance of the Abhidharma will herald the onset of the decline of Buddhism. Hence it was natural to focus first of all on the preservation of the Abhidharma. Meditation practice was taught alongside such Abhidharma teaching activities in order to lead to a direct experience of central tenets of Abhidharma thought.

By this time, tranquillity and insight had come to be seen as two different modes of meditation, rather than complementary qualities as reflected in the early discourses (Anālayo 2003b:

88–91, 2012: 229–235, 2015a: 63–65, and 2017c: 88–107). Given the need to promote insight into Abhidharma, the natural choice was to bypass the cultivation of tranquillity, which was anyway considered less easily accomplishable in the typical living situation of a lay disciple, and to focus on the cultivation of insight.

The emergence of what is known as "dry insight" was based on an understanding of mindfulness as a quality that plunges into the object. Since such plunging into an object involves a considerable degree of focused attention, this to some extent substitutes for the lack of training in concentration proper, as far as the absence of distraction is concerned.

Moreover, mindfulness was by this time seen as intimately bound up with wisdom. Under the overarching concern of inculcating lay followers with basic Abhidharma teachings, a chief purpose of the meditation practice was to lead to an experience of at least some of the ultimate realities as recognized, for example, in a popular Sri Lankan handbook of Abhidharma, the perhaps tenth-century Compendium of Abhidharma (*Abhidhammattha-saṅgaha*). With the development of Abhidharma thought and exegesis, a list of material and mental phenomena had been assembled under the heading of being such ultimate realities. The task of mindfulness then became one of leading to an experience of momentariness and the direct witnessing of the dissolution of mind and matter.

Contemporary insight meditation traditions attempt to achieve this direct experience of momentariness by encouraging a fragmentation of experience, breaking it down into its various components. Slow-motion walking can help to separate the apparent continuity of walking into discrete parts. Labelling of anything experienced serves to foster a realization of the immediate disappearance of whatever has just been noticed. Alternatively, repeated body scanning can lead to an experience of the body's energetic constitution as a mass of vibrations in constant disintegration. Whatever approach is chosen, a chief task of mindfulness remains to lead to the insight knowledge of dissolution (*bhaṅga-ñāṇa*), thereby directly and personally witnessing the dissolution of mind and matter as testifying to the truth of the doctrine of momentariness.

Meditation traditions based on the idea of mindfulness as a quality that plunges into its objects and aimed at a direct experience of momentary dissolution have been remarkably successful and changed the lives of many for the better. Nevertheless, from a historical viewpoint it deserves noting that this is based on an understanding of mindfulness as a quality merged with considerable effort and focus. Although a valid approach, this is not the only possible way of understanding and cultivating mindfulness in order to gain liberating insight.

SUMMARY

As part of an attempt to provide a comprehensive map of the path, instructions on mindfulness shifted from being practice-orientated to becoming doctrine-orientated, in particular serving to actualize the doctrine of momentariness. The quality of mindfulness itself was eventually understood to be intrinsically related to wisdom and to involve a plunging into the object of meditation. These notions combined to yield a form of mindfulness practice aimed at verifying the doctrine of momentariness in the meditator's personal experience of insight.

PRACTICE SUGGESTIONS

In order to explore practically a central dimension of the development depicted in this chapter, contemplation of cessation could be applied to the practice of mindfulness of breathing. Implementing such contemplation requires paying attention to the constantly changing nature of the breath with a keen focus on its recurrent cessation. Every moment in the experience of the breath should be seen as disappearing right on the spot, to make room for the next moment of this experience.

In order to support this mode of practice, some degree of mental labelling can be employed by softly noting "vanishing" or "ceasing" or "ending". In order for such labelling to fulfill its purpose, it is preferable not to overdo it, as this can result in thinking about the endings in each breath rather than experiencing them. Just a brief note to foster clarity of recognition is enough and can be followed by remaining aware of the breath as constantly disappearing, until it seems appropriate to bring in a label once again.

After some time of undertaking this mode of contemplation in relation to the experience of the breath, the same could be carried over into other activities. Throughout, the focus should be on the ending aspect of phenomena with a view to diminishing clinging and attachment to them, in the understanding that it is meaningless to hold on to what is anyway going to pass away.

XII

NON-DUAL MINDFULNESS

This is the last of three chapters on the history of mindfulness. In what follows I proceed from early Buddhism to non-dual forms of mindfulness practice of the type found in Himalayan and East Asian Buddhist meditation traditions. By way of a background to these practices, I first explore the rise of the aspiration to become a Buddha in the future, an aspiration that involves following the path of a "bodhisattva". Another topic to be taken up is the luminosity of the mind and related developments. It is only after exploring these trajectories that I will be able to return to my main topic of mindfulness.

THE BODHISATTVA IDEAL

As mentioned at the outset of the previous chapter, the attribution of omniscience to the Buddha appears to have been a significant factor fuelling an attempt in the Abhidharma traditions to provide as complete a map of the path as possible. However, this is not the only possible reaction to the Buddha's passing away and the resultant need to ensure the continuous availability of Buddhist teachings. Another response would be to try to emulate him by becoming an omniscient teacher oneself in the future.

This alternative revolves around the role of a Buddha, which is to discover the path to awakening and then teach it to others.

The wish to become a Buddha oneself informs the emergence of the bodhisattva ideal, the aspiration of embarking on the gradual progress over a series of lifetimes towards awakening to Buddhahood.

The arising of this alternative model of progress to awakening invests the term "bodhisattva" with a meaning different from its prevalent usage in the early discourses, where it tends to refer mainly to the last life of the Buddha-to-be. The idea that in past lives he had intentionally embarked on the path leading to Buddhahood is clearly a later element. Nevertheless, the early discourses testify to several developments which, in conjunction with other influences, appear to have blazed the trail for the arising of the aspiration to become a Buddha in the future (Anālayo 2010 and 2017a).

A driving force behind several such developments is the tendency to exalt the Buddha. The Discourse on the Marvellous and Wonderful Qualities (of the Buddha) is entirely dedicated to this aim (Anālayo 2011: 702–711). One of several examples of this tendency towards exaltation is a declaration, attributed to the future Buddha at the time of his birth. According to this declaration, just after being born he claimed to be supreme in the world and to have gone beyond future rebirth (Anālayo 2010: 38–46). Comparative study shows this claim to be a later addition. Once this episode had come into being, however, versions of this claim seem to have spread quickly among a range of later traditions and are evident in both texts and art (Anālayo 2011: 709).

The appearance of this passage in the Discourse on the Marvellous and Wonderful Qualities could have simply resulted from borrowing qualities attributed to the Buddha (once he had become such by awakening) and adding these to the list of his marvellous qualities presented in this discourse. Since the Pāli discourse is otherwise concerned with what preceded and what accompanied the future Buddha's birth, it is natural for such a declaration to become associated with the time when he was just born. The net result of such association, however, is that the infant bodhisattva is now invested with a status only achieved once he had grown up and become a Buddha by attaining awakening.

Due to this transfer of qualities from the Buddha to the infant bodhisattva, the status of being a bodhisattva comes to be invested with an intrinsic superiority to anyone else, however much such a bodhisattva's mind is still under the influence of defilements.

This foreshadows a recurrent trope in later texts to extol the superiority of bodhisattvas over those who do not follow this path, whose inferior status serves as a foil against which to demarcate the identity of a practitioner in pursuit of Buddhahood. A particularly striking example of this tendency is the employment of the derogatory term "inferior vehicle" (*hīnayāna*). Although this term is sometimes used in relation to the Buddhists of Sri Lanka, Thailand, and Myanmar, such usage is actually erroneous, since the bodhisattva path is also a recognized part of these traditions, attested in texts, inscriptions, and actual practice. In fact, throughout the history of Buddhism there does not appear to be any identifiable tradition or institution that could rightly be reckoned as belonging to the "inferior vehicle" (Anālayo 2014b). The term appears to be entirely a product of polemic imagination, in line with the basic trajectory of considering a bodhisattva as superior to anyone else.

The same passage from the Discourse on the Marvellous and Wonderful Qualities of the Buddha also sets a precedent for a particular mode of practice among some practitioners of the bodhisattva path. This involves identifying oneself with the state of being a Buddha to the extent of appropriating to one's present condition the qualities that would result from reaching the goal of one's aspiration. In this way, the goal becomes the path, in that progress towards future Buddhahood can take the form of impersonating the qualities of a Buddha as much as possible in the present.

THE LUMINOUS MIND

Another trajectory of considerable importance for appreciating the role of mindfulness in Himalayan and East Asian Buddhist practice traditions is the notion of the mind's inherent luminosity. The early discourses recognize experiences of inner light that result from deepening concentration (Anālayo 2011: 734–738 and 2017g: 32–39). The notion of luminosity as an intrinsic property of the mind, however, appears to be the result of a later development.

This development seems to have started with passages that illustrate the purification of the mind with the example of refining gold. Comparative study makes it fairly probable that, in the course of oral transmission, qualities originally belonging to the gold simile were eventually also applied to the mind. This could have happened quite accidentally as a reciter's error. The net result is that luminosity, as an intrinsic quality of gold, also became an intrinsic quality of the mind (Anālayo 2017f: 20–26). The original idea in this association appears to have been some form of visible luminosity; the idea that the nature of consciousness as such is to illumine its objects appears to be a later development.

Once this association had become established, a further stage of development seems to be reflected in a passage in the Numerical Collection, which speaks of the luminous mind that is with and without adventitious defilements (Anālayo 2017f: 26–36). The imagery in this discourse is clearly indebted to the gold-refining simile. Taken on its own, however, the discourse conveys the impression that the mind is luminous even when defilements are present. In early Buddhist thought, however, such a condition of the mind would require that defilements are at least temporarily in abeyance and the mind has become concentrated.

An Abhidharma work has an apparent quotation of this passage, with the difference that this version speaks of the mind as being intrinsically "pure". Once arisen, this idea of an intrinsically pure and luminous condition of the mind had a lasting influence on subsequent texts, leading eventually to the notion that the mind is already purified and awakened (Anālayo 2017f: 36–43). In some traditions, this luminous mind was in turn identified with the so-called "store-house consciousness" (*ālaya-vijñāna*). This special type of consciousness stores, as it were, the seeds from the past, which thus can later be remembered (another response to the problem posed by momentariness for appreciating the functioning of memory).

This notion of an already awakened condition of the mind significantly changes the way meditation practice was in turn conceptualized. In early Buddhist thought, the starting point for mental cultivation is a mind that has been defiled since time immemorial and now needs to be gradually purified. Once the mind is seen as already awakened since time immemorial, however, mental cultivation instead has the task of becoming aware of this already awakened condition.

The need to aid the meditation student in reaching such recognition of the intrinsically pure and luminous mind informs various skilful means, such as cryptic sayings, unexpected actions, or just silent abiding in meditation. In one way or another, thought activity in the mind needs to be stilled in order to enable the non-dual experience of the true nature of the mind to manifest itself.

THE NATURE OF THE MIND

Experiencing the mind as such is, at least to some degree, already found in early Buddhist teachings. Non-dual experiences can be accessed through the attainment of different levels of concentrative absorption, which in themselves already convey some form of experiencing the mind as such (Gethin forthcoming). Based on the attainment of the four levels of concentrative absorption described in the discourses, the so-called immaterial spheres can be cultivated. The second of these immaterial spheres involves the experience of boundless consciousness. Here the mind is aware just of itself, after having reached a boundless condition through having earlier attended to boundless space. The experience of the second immaterial sphere can result in a powerful mode of abiding in knowing the mind as such.

The experience of the mind as such is not confined to the cultivation of deep absorption. This can be seen in a series of perceptions that form part of a gradual entry into emptiness, described in the Smaller Discourse on Emptiness (Anālayo 2011: 683–688 and 2015a: 83–150). One of the meditative steps in this gradual entry into emptiness involves precisely the "perception" of boundless consciousness; another step is the experience of signlessness (*animitta*). Such meditative steps resemble in several ways experiences related to the nature of the mind in later traditions.

A significant difference, however, is that such early Buddhist precedents carry no implication of revealing an intrinsic state of purity, let alone a level of awakening already attained. Instead, they are simply part of a series of meditative steps that can lead to liberation. In early Buddhist thought, to affirm emptiness is at the same time an affirmation of conditionality and impermanence.

In this way, whereas the experience of the mind as such appears to be part of the meditative repertoire of early Buddhism, an interpretation of such experiences as revealing an intrinsically pure, luminous, and already awakened condition of the mind appears to be a later development.

Such a development would have had a more widespread appeal in an environment where notions of inherent superiority were already well established. This applies to the evolving bodhisattva ideal and its attribution of inherent superiority to those who follow the path to future Buddhahood over any other practitioner, however much the mind of a bodhisattva may still be under the influence of defilements. This is even more the case once impersonating in the present what is to be reached with full awakening had come to be an accepted mode of practice. In such a setting, the notion of a mind intrinsically awakened and luminous, even when defilements are present, would easily have gained acceptance. In fact, it involves the same inversion of the conditional relationship between path and goal. Whereas in early Buddhist thought cultivating the noble eightfold path is the cause for eventually reaching the goal, now the goal, as an already inherent quality of the mind, becomes the cause for the path of recognizing and enacting this goal.

MOMENTARINESS AND EMPTINESS

Another significant development, relevant to my present exploration, relates to implications of the doctrine of momentariness. In a way, positing that something disappears right after it has arisen could still seem to be involving two distinct moments, one of arising and the second one of disappearing. In order to be able to reduce this to a single moment, arising and disappearing will have to be considered as taking place at the same time. In this way, once the notion of momentariness was taken to its extreme, any duration of phenomena came to be denied and their entire existence was effaced (von Rospatt 1995: 80).

The teaching that things are "not permanent" was re-interpreted as stating that they are "permanently not", in the sense that they are so thoroughly empty that from the outset they do not have any existence (von Rospatt 1995: 71). Once something has no duration, it easily follows that no change can be predicated of it. In this way, the relationship between the characteristics of impermanence and emptiness (in the sense of the absence of a permanent self) was severed and the first of these two characteristics had to leave the stage to make room for a thoroughgoing emphasis on emptiness. Whereas in early Buddhist thought the mind is considered to be empty of a self precisely because it is impermanent, in some strands of this later current of thought the mind is no longer viewed as impermanent precisely because it is so thoroughly empty.

Another relevant current of thought emerged out of reflections on the memory nuance of mindfulness. This contrasts with the line of interpretation described in the previous chapter, which led to conceiving mindfulness as invariably wholesome and connected with wisdom. In another Abhidharma tradition, the reasoning instead emerged that mindfulness must be present in every state of mind, simply because otherwise it would be impossible to remember this state at a later time (Cox 1992/1993: 83f and 88). This then led to the position that mindfulness is present in any mental experience, rather than being a quality that needs to be intentionally cultivated.

From the viewpoint of early Buddhist thought, a quality present in any state of mind is attention (*manasikāra*). Hence, in the case of attention the task is not so much its cultivation as such, but rather how attention is directed. This can be penetrative and wise or else superficial and unwise (see Anālayo 2009b and 2020a).

A comparable shift of perspective results once mindfulness was considered to be always present. On that premise, there is no longer a need to devote time and effort to cultivating mindfulness as such. Instead, the more imperative question becomes in what way such mindfulness is being deployed.

Influenced in one way or another by the strands of thought depicted above, in several practice traditions mindfulness came to serve as the tool for recognizing the nature of the mind. Such recognition and practice is less about something to be cultivated, but much rather about something inherent that reveals itself once other mental activities subside.

The need for mindfulness to lead to a direct experience of the nature of the mind is evident among practice traditions related to the Great Perfection (Kapstein 1992/1993) and the Zen/Chán traditions (Sharf 2014). In order to achieve this direct encounter with the nature of the mind, mindfulness itself has to remain completely free from conceptual thought activity and take on a non-dual quality, in the sense of avoiding the trap of creating a subject–object duality (Dunne 2011). Given that mindfulness is not considered a quality to be actively cultivated, there is a recurrent emphasis on non-fabrication, even non-meditation.

The Great Perfection and the Zen/Chán traditions offer powerful approaches to mental cultivation that can have a range of benefits. Nevertheless, it needs to be kept in mind that the notion of mindfulness in these traditions is not the only possible way of cultivating mindfulness in order to realize the empty nature of the mind.

SUMMARY

The gradual evolution of the bodhisattva ideal, with its assumption of an intrinsic superiority, provided the appropriate stage for an association of luminosity with the nature of the mind to evolve into the notion that the mind is intrinsically pure and already awakened. With this notion in place, the task of mindfulness, by now seen in some traditions as a quality present in any state of mind, became one of recognition of this already awakened nature. For this purpose, mindfulness had to stay aloof from concepts and the subject–object duality.

It thereby became substantially different from, even the opposite of, the type of mindfulness required in the insight traditions aimed at a direct experience of momentariness, discussed in the previous chapter. Each of these two constructs of mindfulness has an antecedent in early Buddhist thought. At the same time, each has developed further and taken on its own characteristic understanding of what mindfulness is and how it should be employed.

PRACTICE SUGGESTIONS

The recommendation for a meditation practice reflecting topics explored in the present chapter would be to employ mindfulness of breathing to discern the mind as such. This requires turning back or inwards, as it were, from being aware of the breath to that which is aware, that which knows the breath: the flow of consciousness.

This can be distinguished from the more active dimensions of the meditative experience, which are the material dimension of the flow of the breath and the mental dimension in the discerning of this breath as an inhalation or an exhalation. Letting go of such discerning for the time being, attention can turn to that part of the mind which just knows, that which is just aware.

Once meditative practice has led to a recognition of the mind as such, the same practice can be related to everyday situations. In any situation it is in principle possible to step back internally from active involvement and just be with the receptivity of bare knowing, of resting in the experience of the mind as such.

CONCLUSION

In what follows, I briefly survey central dimensions of mindfulness in early Buddhist thought that have emerged in the course of the previous twelve chapters. From a quick recap of the historical development surveyed in the last two chapters, I turn to the current employment of mindfulness in a range of arenas in secular society. In the final part of this conclusion, I relate the potential of mindfulness to the current ecological and climatic crisis on this planet.

DIMENSIONS OF MINDFULNESS

Key aspects of mindfulness are learning to be more fully in touch with what takes place instead of acting in autopilot mode, remaining in the present instead of mentally wandering off, and learning to slow down and come to our senses. Receptivity to the present moment can be related to the memory nuance of mindfulness, since being fully with the here and now makes it easier to recall later what happened.

Besides being directed within, mindfulness can be applied externally as well, in the sense of discerning how what happens impacts others. Such external deployment of mindfulness will naturally tend to strengthen our concern to maintain and improve the kind of ethical conduct that avoids harming others and ourselves, a concern that lies at the core of compassion. The breadth of vision that results from cultivating mindfulness internally and externally also relates to compassion, which can similarly foster a broad, open-minded, and even boundless mental attitude.

In daily life, an anchor of mindfulness can be established in the body through awareness of our bodily posture. This can serve to counter distraction and the tendency towards fragmentation in sensory experience. Embodied mindfulness cultivated in this way reveals both a grounding quality of mindfulness and its role of providing protection. Mindfulness protects oneself and others by introducing a moment of simple receptive openness before reacting, thereby enabling us to take informed action rather than blindly acting out our first impulses.

In early Buddhist thought, mindfulness can be "right", in the sense of being supportive for progress to awakening, and "wrong", in the sense of being opposed to the same. In addition, some modalities of mindfulness do not seem to fall neatly into either of these two categories.

Although mindfulness is so versatile that it can collaborate with a range of other mental qualities, including focused attention, on its own mindfulness does not come with an exclusive focus. Instead, it is more of an inclusive quality, characterized by a breadth of vision rather than a narrow focal point. The idea that mindfulness plunges into its object is a later development.

When cultivated in the form of four establishments, mindfulness comes with a clear emphasis on the present moment and is concerned with overcoming desires and discontent. In the context of the four establishments, mindfulness collaborates with diligence and clear knowing; the latter is responsible for engendering meditative wisdom through the skilful employment of concepts for the purpose of clarity of understanding.

A particular modality of mindfulness takes the form of bare awareness. This can help to discern, and to some extent counter, the constructing nature of the mind, evident in perceptual prediction. With mindfulness established, it becomes possible to avoid the mind becoming afflicted when the body is afflicted, and to learn to face mortality. The latter can counter two strategies of denial, by bringing home the fact that death affects all of us and that it could even happen right now.

The Buddha is on record for having taken the challenge of mortality seriously enough to set out in search of the deathless. During his quest for awakening, the potential of mindfulness appears to have become clear to him in various ways. Key aspects seem to have been awareness of postures, monitoring the impact of feeling tones, recognition of the condition of the mind (distinguished into wholesome and unwholesome types), and a practical exploration of the conditionality of the mind. All of the contributions made by mindfulness to the Buddha's own progress to awakening would have led to the central role mindfulness was to take in his teachings. This role evolves from its pre-Buddhist precedents, where mindfulness had a central but not exclusive relationship to memory, or better, to "keeping in mind". In its early Buddhist usage, mindfulness features in a variety of contexts and applications, making it a versatile and adaptable mental quality.

A HISTORY OF MINDFULNESS

The developments surveyed in the last two chapters show the arising of two significant perspectives on mindfulness in later Buddhist tradition. In one of these, mindfulness came to be understood as invariably wholesome and intrinsically related to wisdom. Moreover, mindfulness was seen as involving a plunging into the object of meditation practice, whose purpose was to enable a direct experience of the momentary nature of reality. In the other, mindfulness was instead seen as a quality present in any state of mind. Here mindfulness has to stay aloof from concepts and the subject–object duality in order to enable a recognition of the already awakened nature of the mind.

Now some degree of cessation can indeed be experienced at every moment in the mind, otherwise there would be no room for something new to arise and be cognized. Yet, continuity in the mind is also experienced at all times, otherwise any learning from the past becomes impossible. In this way, each of these two perspectives is a partial truth and fails to encompass the complete picture.

In both cases, mindfulness serves to confirm the respective doctrinal perspective, be it the momentary or the luminous nature of the mind. In order to fulfil this function, mindfulness necessarily has to be circumscribed. Either it has to involve discrimination and concepts or else it must dispense with both. Either it needs be actively pursuing an object in a methodical manner or else it has to remain uninvolved to the point of being completely aloof from any method or object.

Each of these two constructs of mindfulness has developed from an antecedent in early Buddhist thought, subsequently taking on its own characteristic understanding of what mindfulness is and how it should be deployed. The same holds for contemporary mindfulness used in the clinical setting and education, etc. This, too, has adopted aspects of early Buddhism, explored in Chapter 1 on mindful eating and in Chapter 8 on healing, developed these further, and formulated its own characteristic understanding.

Contemporary mindfulness in secular usage differs from the two constructs of mindfulness discussed in the last two chapters. It lacks the discriminating dimension of the insight tradition and also the non-dual absence of concepts. Instead of being a further development of either of these two, it is yet another independent branch growing out of the roots of early Buddhism.

The different constructs of mindfulness that have emerged in the course of time could be compared to different parts of an elephant. A well-known simile describes several blind persons each touching a particular part of an elephant, such as its tail, its legs, or its ears (Anālayo 2017b: 163n102). When questioned about the nature of an elephant, the blind persons each present their own particular view, grounded in personal and direct experience. Not realizing the limitations of their respective personal experience, the blind persons start quarrelling with each other about who got it right.

Quarrelling about the "right" definition of mindfulness by privileging one of these constructs over the other would be similar to the predicament of these blind persons. Adopting a historical perspective by seeing their similarities and differences as results of a gradual evolution can help transcend the limited view that leads to contention. There is nothing wrong in taking hold of the part of the elephant that is within reach in order to have a direct experience of it. A problem only arises when the part is mistaken for the whole.

GLOBALIZATION OF MINDFULNESS

Having spread around the globe and into a range of different parts of society, mindfulness offers a timely tool to face the current ecological and climatic crisis (Anālayo 2019i and 2019l). The destruction of the environment and climate change have reached dimensions that, if unchecked, will eventually threaten the very survival of humanity on this planet. The possible future scenarios are truly devastating: oceans turning acidic and fish dying, extinction of the majority of animal species, large areas of fertile land turning into deserts or being flooded by the ocean, massive depletion of drinking water supplies, crop failure, large-scale migration and warfare in competition for dwindling resources. Such scenarios are so horrible that we would rather not even think about them. Yet, avoiding thinking about them is one of the factors contributing to the present crisis.

Here mindfulness can offer a much-needed solution. It can become a central tool to enable us to face the horror and take the steps needed to transform what might well be the most serious challenge human beings have ever faced in their history into a great opportunity: an opportunity to raise the level of global awareness and move to a level of interaction among human beings that gives precedence to the common welfare over the individual benefit. The challenge posed by the crisis, if handled with mindfulness on a broad scale, can become an opportunity to work together to maintain the living conditions required for the survival of human civilization. This requires stepping out of the narrow confines of self-centredness, based on rigidly held racial, political, religious, and social identities. At this stage, it is no longer possible to privilege the individual over the communal, the regional over the national, and the national over the international. Instead, we must come to appreciate what we all have in common, the potential to become what so far we have not yet really become: *homo sapiens sapiens*, truly "wise" human beings.

To actualize our human potential requires the support of mindfulness to enable a stepping out of three types of reaction to the crisis: denial, anger, and resignation. I propose to map these to the three root defilements recognized in early Buddhism: greed, aversion, and delusion.

When faced with information about ecological destruction and climate change with their potential repercussions, it is a natural reaction of the untrained mind to want to avoid and forget about it, in order to be able to continue enjoying the pleasures of this world without having to worry too much about the consequences. In this way denial, which I consider to be predominantly an expression of the root defilement of greed, prevents us from reacting appropriately to what is happening. The forces of greed are strong enough to have made denial an intentionally cultivated strategy by leading politicians and high-level executives of companies who would be affected if action were taken to prevent a worsening of the crisis. A common mode of such denial is to pretend that the information we have is not sufficiently well established to be taken seriously.

Yet, we have regular reports by international committees of scientists, which summarize our current level of knowledge. There can be no doubt that the situation is serious and that it demands swift action. Note that it is enough for us to know that a threat is probable; we do not need to be absolutely certain. This is part of how our perception works, which involves "perceptual prediction" (see above p. 73). On suddenly seeing a dangerous animal in front of us, we will react on the spot. We cannot afford to wait until all possible information about the animal has been gathered and we are completely sure that it is indeed intent on attacking us, since by then it may be too late. Similarly, faced by the probable outcomes of the current crisis, it is time to act now, before it is too late.

This remains a challenge for each of us, as long as the forces of the root defilements are still present in our minds. The tendency to want to avoid and forget about it all can exert a strong influence that is hardly noticed, unless mindfulness is established. From this viewpoint, the global crisis can become an opportunity for mindfully scrutinizing our own mind in order to detect the potential influence of the root defilement of greed, however subtly it might manifest, in fostering denial.

The second type of reaction is anger. As just mentioned, some leading politicians and high-level executives are actively working to prevent appropriate changes from taking place. Yet, getting angry with them is not a solution. For one, we are all part of the problem, even if unintendedly. Let the one of us who has never driven a car, taken a plane, eaten food imported from abroad, worn clothing manufactured in a distant country, etc., throw the first stone.

Besides, I fail to see a place for righteous anger in early Buddhist thought. There is definitely a place for stern and strong action, but this should come with inner balance. If we operate from a position of inner balance, sooner or later it becomes clear to us that those "bad ones" in politics and economy are in the end simply in a condition of being at the mercy of defilements. They do not know what they are doing.

From the viewpoint of mindfulness practice, getting angry at them is not the appropriate response, because in doing so we succumb to one of the root defilements and thereby to what has led to and sustains the crisis. Anger is a problem and not a solution. A solution can be found only when the mind is unhindered by defilements, at least temporarily, and therefore able to know and see things accurately. The present situation, within and without, calls for mindfulness in combination with clarity of understanding, embedded in the right intention of non-harm. These are the appropriate qualities with which to face our internal responses and to counteract those external manifestations of the root defilements that are related in one way or another to a deterioration of living conditions on earth.

The third type of reaction is resignation, which I relate to the root defilement of delusion. It manifests in a sense of feeling overwhelmed and helpless. As a single individual, it just seems so hopeless to try to effect any change. What is the point of even trying? Yet, society is made up of individuals and does not exist apart from them. The question is not whether a single individual can bring about all required change alone. The question is rather whether every single individual can contribute to the required change. This is indeed the case.

From this viewpoint, the small steps we might take in our daily lives acquire significance as an embodiment of our mindfulness practice. Be it living more simply, shifting to a vegetarian diet, recycling, or forgoing unnecessary travel. All of these become meaningful not because the world will change if one individual acts in this way. They become meaningful because they embody our awareness of the global crisis and express it on the individual level as a form of training in mindfulness.

Of course, the more of us who act in this way, the greater the effects will be. This ties in with the internal and external dimensions of mindfulness. It is precisely through embodying what needs to be done on the personal level that the external level can be positively affected. In this way, the quality of protection inherent in mindfulness can become the way to protect ourselves and others.

Just as mindfulness enables us to be with physical pain without either switching off or else resisting, similarly mindfulness can ease the mental pain of facing the horror of what we human beings are doing to ourselves. This is the first and most important foundational step. It is by training ourselves to be able to face the crisis with mindfulness that we will be able to share this attitude with others and inspire them to cultivate the same, and it is based on this attitude that any ecological activism to confront the crisis has the greatest potential.

Just as mindfulness can gradually expand into accompanying various daily activities, so we can expand our awareness to embodying our understanding in various ways. Just as mindfulness has internal and external dimensions, similarly our ability to learn to face the current ecological and climatic crisis can find expression in a variety of ways and activities. Each of us can find our own suitable ways to embody how the crisis is best faced: with mindfulness.

REFERENCES

Amaro, Ajahn 2015: "A Holistic Mindfulness", *Mindfulness*, 6: 63–73.

Anālayo, Bhikkhu 2003a: "Nimitta", in *Encyclopaedia of Buddhism*, W.G. Weeraratne (ed.), 7.4: 177–179, Sri Lanka: Department of Buddhist Affairs.

— 2003b: *Satipaṭṭhāna, The Direct Path to Realization*, Birmingham: Windhorse Publications.

— 2009a: "Yodhājīva Sutta", in *Encyclopaedia of Buddhism*, W.G. Weeraratne (ed.), 8.3: 789–799, Sri Lanka: Department of Buddhist Affairs.

— 2009b: "Yonisomanasikāra", in *Encyclopaedia of Buddhism*, W.G. Weeraratne (ed.), 8.3: 809–815, Sri Lanka: Department of Buddhist Affairs (reprinted in 2012).

— 2010: *The Genesis of the Bodhisattva Ideal*, Hamburg: Hamburg University Press.

— 2011: *A Comparative Study of the Majjhima nikāya*, Taipei: Dharma Drum Publishing Corporation.

— 2012: *Excursions into the Thought-world of the Pāli Discourses*, Onalaska WA: Pariyatti.

— 2013: *Perspectives on Satipaṭṭhāna*, Cambridge: Windhorse Publications.

— 2014a: *The Dawn of Abhidharma*, Hamburg: Hamburg University Press.

— 2014b: "The Hīnayāna Fallacy", *Journal of the Oxford Centre for Buddhist Studies*, 6: 9–31 (reprinted in 2016a).

— 2015a: *Compassion and Emptiness in Early Buddhist Meditation*, Cambridge: Windhorse Publications.

— 2015b: "Compassion in the Āgamas and Nikāyas", *Dharma Drum Journal of Buddhist Studies*, 16: 1–30.

— 2015c: *Saṃyukta-āgama Studies*, Taipei: Dharma Drum Publishing Corporation.

— 2016a: *Ekottarika-āgama Studies*, Taipei: Dharma Drum Publishing Corporation.

— 2016b: *Mindfully Facing Disease and Death, Compassionate Advice from Early Buddhist Texts*, Cambridge: Windhorse Publications.

— 2017a: *Buddhapada and the Bodhisattva Path*, Bochum: Projektverlag.

— 2017b: *Dīrgha-āgama Studies*, Taipei: Dharma Drum Publishing Corporation.

— 2017c: *Early Buddhist Meditation Studies*, Barre: Barre Center for Buddhist Studies.

— 2017d: "The Healing Potential of the Awakening Factors in Early Buddhist Discourse", in *Buddhism and Medicine, An Anthology of Premodern Sources*, C.P. Salguero (ed.), 12–19, New York: Columbia University Press.

— 2017e: "How Compassion Became Painful", *Journal of the Centre for Buddhist Studies, Sri Lanka*, 14: 85–113.

— 2017f: "The Luminous Mind in Theravāda and Dharmaguptaka Discourses", *Journal of the Oxford Centre for Buddhist Studies*, 13: 10–51.

— 2017g: *A Meditator's Life of the Buddha, Based on the Early Discourses*, Cambridge: Windhorse Publications.

— 2018a: "The Bāhiya Instruction and Bare Awareness", *Indian International Journal of Buddhist Studies*, 19: 1–19.

— 2018b: "The Influxes and Mindful Eating", *Insight Journal*, 44: 31–42.

— 2018c: "Mindfulness Constructs in Early Buddhism and Theravāda, Another Contribution to the Memory Debate", *Mindfulness*, 9.4: 1047–1051.

— 2018d: "Once again on Mindfulness and Memory", *Mindfulness*, 9.1: 1–6.

— 2018e: "Overeating and Mindfulness in Ancient India", *Mindfulness*, 9.5: 1648–1654.

— 2018f: "The Potential of Facing Anger with Mindfulness", *Mindfulness*, 9.6: 1966–1972.

— 2018g: *Rebirth in Early Buddhism and Contemporary Research*, Boston: Wisdom Publications.

— 2018h: "Remembering with Wisdom Is Not Intrinsic to All Forms of Mindfulness", *Mindfulness*, 9.6: 1987–1990.

— 2018i: *Satipaṭṭhāna Meditation: A Practice Guide*, Cambridge: Windhorse Publications.

— 2018j: "Why Be Mindful of Feelings?", *Contemporary Buddhism*, 19.1: 47–53.

— 2019a: "Adding Historical Depth to Definitions of Mindfulness", *Current Opinion in Psychology*, 28: 11–14.

— 2019b: "Ancient Indian Education and Mindfulness", *Mindfulness*, 10.5: 964–969.

— 2019c: "Definitions of Right Concentration in Comparative Perspective", *Singaporean Journal of Buddhist Studies*, 5: 9–39.

— 2019d: "The Emphasis on the Present Moment in the Cultivation of Mindfulness", *Mindfulness*, 10.3: 571–581.

— 2019e: "Food and Insight", *Insight Journal*, 45: 1–10.

— 2019f: "How Mindfulness Came to Plunge into Its Objects", *Mindfulness*, 10.6: 1181–1185.

— 2019g: "Immeasurable Meditations and Mindfulness", *Mindfulness*, 10.12: 2620–2628.

— 2019h: "In the Seen just the Seen: Mindfulness and the Construction of Experience", *Mindfulness*, 10.1: 179–184.

— 2019i: *Mindfully Facing Climate Change*, Barre: Barre Center for Buddhist Studies.

— 2019j: *Mindfulness of Breathing: A Practice Guide and Translations*, Cambridge: Windhorse Publications.

— 2019k: "The Role of Mindfulness in the Cultivation of Absorption", *Mindfulness*, 10.11: 2341–2351.

— 2019l: "A Task for Mindfulness: Facing Climate Change", *Mindfulness*, 10.9: 1926–1935.

— 2020a: "Attention and Mindfulness", *Mindfulness*, 11.

— 2020b: "External Mindfulness", *Mindfulness*, 11.

— 2020c: "Gotama Buddha", in *The Routledge Handbook of Indian Buddhist Philosophy*, W. Edelglass, S. McClintock, and P. Harter (ed.), forthcoming.

— 2020d. *Mindfulness in Early Buddhism. Characteristics and Functions*, Cambridge: Windhorse Publications.

Brown, Erik 2013: *The Birth of Insight: Meditation, Modern Buddhism and the Burmese Monk Ledi Sayadaw*, Chicago: University of Chicago Press.

Collett, Alice and Bh. Anālayo 2014: "Bhikkhave and Bhikkhu as Gender-inclusive Terminology in Early Buddhist Texts", *Journal of Buddhist Ethics*, 21: 760–797.

Cox, Collett 1992/1993: "Mindfulness and Memory: The Scope of Smṛti from Early Buddhism to the Sarvāstivādin Abhidharma", in *In the Mirror of Memory, Reflections on Mindfulness and Remembrance in Indian and Tibetan Buddhism*, J. Gyatso (ed.), 67–108, Delhi: Sri Satguru.

Dunne, John 2011: "Toward an Understanding of Non-dual Mindfulness", *Contemporary Buddhism*, 12.1: 71–88.

Gethin, Rupert 1992: *The Buddhist Path to Awakening: A Study of the Bodhi-Pakkhiyā Dhammā*, Leiden: E.J. Brill.

— (forthcoming): "Jhānas and the Path to Liberation", Avila.

Gunaratana, Henepola 1991/1992: *Mindfulness in Plain English*, Boston: Wisdom Publications.

Kabat-Zinn, Jon 1990/2013: *Full Catastrophe Living: Using the Wisdom of Your Body and Mind to Face Stress, Pain, and Illness,* New York: Bantam Books.

Kapstein, Matthew 1992/1993: "The Amnesic Monarch and the Five Mnemic Men: 'Memory' in Great Perfection (Rdzogs-chen) Thought", in *In the Mirror of Memory, Reflections on Mindfulness and Remembrance in Indian and Tibetan Buddhism,* J. Gyatso (ed.), 239–269, Delhi: Sri Satiguru.

Klaus, Konrad 1993: "On the Meaning of the Root smṛ in Vedic literature", *Wiener Zeitschrift für die Kunde Südasiens,* 36: 77–86.

Monier-Williams, M. 1899/1999: *A Sanskrit–English Dictionary, Etymologically and Philologically Arranged, With Special Reference to Cognate Indo-European Languages,* Delhi: Motilal Banarsidass.

Sharf, Robert 2014: "Mindfulness and Mindlessness in Early Chan", *Philosophy East and West,* 64.4: 933–964.

von Rospatt, Alexander 1995: *The Buddhist Doctrine of Momentariness: A Survey of the Origins and Early Phase of this Doctrine up to Vasubandhu,* Stuttgart: Franz Steiner Verlag.

INDEX

WINDHORSE PUBLICATIONS

Windhorse Publications is a Buddhist charitable company based in the UK. We place great emphasis on producing books of high quality that are accessible and relevant to those interested in Buddhism at whatever level. We are the main publisher of the works of Sangharakshita, the founder of the Triratna Buddhist Order and Community. Our books draw on the whole range of the Buddhist tradition, including translations of traditional texts, commentaries, books that make links with contemporary culture and ways of life, biographies of Buddhists, and works on meditation.

As a not-for-profit enterprise, we ensure that all surplus income is invested in new books and improved production methods, to better communicate Buddhism in the 21st century. We welcome donations to help us continue our work – to find out more, go to windhorsepublications.com.

The Windhorse is a mythical animal that flies over the earth carrying on its back three precious jewels, bringing these invaluable gifts to all humanity: the Buddha (the 'awakened one'), his teaching, and the community of all his followers.

Windhorse Publications
info@windhorsepublications.com

Perseus Distribution
210 American Drive
Jackson TN 38301
USA

Windhorse Books
PO Box 574
Newtown NSW 2042
Australia

THE TRIRATNA BUDDHIST COMMUNITY

Windhorse Publications is a part of the Triratna Buddhist Community, an international movement with centres in Europe, India, North and South America and Australasia. At these centres, members of the Triratna Buddhist Order offer classes in meditation and Buddhism. Activities of the Triratna Community also include retreat centres, residential spiritual communities, ethical Right Livelihood businesses, and the Karuna Trust, a UK fundraising charity that supports social welfare projects in the slums and villages of India.

Through these and other activities, Triratna is developing a unique approach to Buddhism, not simply as a philosophy and a set of techniques, but as a creatively directed way of life for all people living in the conditions of the modern world.

If you would like more information about Triratna please visit thebuddhistcentre.com or write to:

London Buddhist Centre
51 Roman Road
London E2 0HU
UK

Aryaloka
14 Heartwood Circle
Newmarket NH 03857
USA

Sydney Buddhist Centre
24 Enmore Road
Sydney NSW 2042
Australia

Also from Windhorse Publications

Satipaṭṭhāna: the direct path to realization

Bhikkhu Anālayo

This best-selling book offers a unique and detailed textual study of the Satipaṭṭhāna Sutta, a foundational Buddhist discourse on meditation practice.

This book should prove to be of value both to scholars of Early Buddhism and to serious meditators alike. – Bhikku Bodhi

. . . a gem . . . I learned a lot from this wonderful book and highly recommend it. – Joseph Goldstein

An indispensible guide . . . surely destined to become the classic commentary on the Satipaṭṭhāna. – Christopher Titmuss

Very impressive and useful, with its blend of strong scholarship and attunement to practice issues. – Prof. Peter Harvey, author of *An Introduction to Buddhist Ethics*

ISBN 9781 899579 54 9 | £17.99 / $28.95 / €19.95 | 336 pages

A Meditator's Life of the Buddha: based on the early discourses

Bhikkhu Anālayo

The author offers an inspiring biography of the Buddha based on the early discourses. By focusing on his meditative development and practice – on the Buddha as a meditator – Bhikkhu Anālayo seeks to provide inspiration and guidance to all meditators, of any tradition and any level of experience. Each of the twenty-four chapters concludes with suggestions to support meditative practice.

While offering a scholarly portrait of the Buddha, this book is also a testament to the overarching unity of the various early Buddhist schools in their conception of the Buddha's life, a unity that coexists along with a rich diversity in their detailed narrations about particular events in that life. – Bhikkhu Bodhi, scholar and translator

An inspiring guide that will accelerate the reader's own journey of awakening. Highly recommended, and sure to inspire dedicated meditators! – Shaila Catherine, author of *Focused and Fearless: A Meditator's Guide to States of Deep Joy, Calm, and Clarity*

ISBN 978 1 909314 99 3 | £13.99 / $19.95 / €16.95 | 280 pages

Compassion and Emptiness in Early Buddhist Meditation

Bhikkhu Anālayo

Exploring the meditative practices of compassion and emptiness, Bhikkhu Anālayo casts fresh light on their earliest sources in the Buddhist tradition.

This book is the result of rigorous textual scholarship that can be valued not only by the academic community, but also by Buddhist practitioners. This book serves as an important bridge between those who wish to learn about Buddhist thought and practice and those who wish to learn from it. As a monk engaging himself in Buddhist meditation as well as a professor applying a historical-critical methodology, Bhikkhu Anālayo is well positioned to bridge these two communities. – 17th Karmapa Ogyen Trinley Dorje

In this study, Venerable Anālayo brings a meticulous textual analysis of Pali texts, the Chinese Āgamas and related material from Sanskrit and Tibetan to the foundational topics of compassion and emptiness. While his analysis is grounded in a scholarly approach, he has written this study as a helpful guide for meditation practice. – Jetsunma Tenzin Palmo

This is an intriguing and delightful book that presents these topics from the viewpoint of the early suttas as well as from other perspectives, and grounds them in both theory and meditative practice. – Bhikshuni Thubten Chodron

Anālayo holds a lamp to illuminate how the earliest teachings wed the great heart of compassion and the liberating heart of emptiness and invites us to join in this profound training. – Jack Kornfield

This scholarly book is more than timely with its demonstrations that teachings on emptiness and compassion that are helpful to practitioners of any form of Buddhism are abundant in early Buddhist texts. – Rita M. Gross

Arising from the author's long-term, dedicated practice and study, this book provides a window into the depth and beauty of the Buddha's liberating teachings. Serious meditation students will benefit tremendously from the clarity of understanding that Venerable Anālayo's efforts have achieved. – Sharon Salzberg

ISBN 978 1 909314 55 9 | £13.99 / $19.95 / €16.95 | 232 pages

Mindfully Facing Disease and Death: compassionate advice from early Buddhist texts

Bhikkhu Anālayo

This unique anthology from the Buddha's early discourses focuses on guidance for facing disease and death, and has the overarching theme of *anukampā*: compassion as the underlying motivation in altruistic action.

The author draws on his own translations from the Chinese *Āgama* collection, presented here for the first time, alongside their counterparts from the Pāli texts, enabling readers to compare the parallel versions in English translation. Taken together with Bhikkhu Anālayo's practical commentary we gain a first-hand impression of what early Buddhism had to say about disease and death.

These teachings invite us to integrate their guidance directly into the laboratory of our own meditation practice and life, in the spirit of deep investigation and inquiry. As committed meditation practitioners know first hand, there is no more worthy or meaningful introspective undertaking in the world, nor a more difficult challenge for human beings to adopt and sustain throughout life. – From the Foreword, Jon Kabat-Zinn

An invaluable and extraordinary resource on the profound teachings by the Buddha on dying, death, and grieving. Bhikkhu Anālayo has given a great gift to all of us by bringing together in this book the compassionate wisdom of the Buddha on our mortality. – Roshi Joan Halifax

This is an indispensable book for serious students of Buddhism. It has the potential to transform the lives of everyone who reads it. – Toni Bernhard

I believe the Buddha would rejoice in this book and exhort all of us to read it and apply the medicine within. This will help to bring about the deepest healing of all – the healing of the mind and the heart – even if we are slipping over the final frontier of death itself. – Vidyamala Burch

ISBN 978 1 909314 72 6 | £13.99 / $19.95 / €16.95 | 320 pages

Satipaṭṭhāna Meditation: a practice guide

Bhikkhu Anālayo

Buddhist meditator and scholar Bhikkhu Anālayo presents this thorough-going guide to the early Buddhist teachings on *Satipaṭṭhāna*, the foundations of mindfulness, following on from his two best-selling books, *Satipaṭṭhāna* and *Perspectives on Satipaṭṭhāna*. With mindfulness being so widely taught, there is a need for a clear-sighted and experience-based guide.

Anālayo provides inspiration and guidance to all meditators, of any tradition and any level of experience. Each of the twenty-four chapters concludes with suggestions to support meditative practice.

This is a pearl of a book. The wise and experienced teacher is offering Dhamma reflections, illuminating the practice of Satipaṭṭhāna *with a fertile and colourful lucidity. It is a treasure-house of practical teachings, rendered accessible with a clear and simple eloquence, and with praiseworthy skill and grace. –* Ajahn Amaro

This breathtaking Practice Guide *is brief, and profound! It offers a detailed, engaging, and flexible approach to* Satipaṭṭhāna *meditation that can be easily applied both in meditation and day to day activities. –* Shaila Catherine, author of *Focused and Fearless: A Meditator's Guide to States of Deep Joy, Calm, and Clarity*

Once more Bhikkhu Anālayo has written a masterpiece that holds within it an accessible and clear guide to developing and applying the teachings held within the Satipaṭṭhāna-sutta. *–* Christina Feldman, author of *The Boundless Heart*

Anālayo has developed a simple and straightforward map of practice instructions encompassing all four satipaṭṭhānas *– the body, feelings, mind and* dharmas *– that build upon one another in a coherent and comprehensive path leading to the final goal. –* Joseph Goldstein, co-founder of the Insight Meditation Society, from the Foreword

Bhikkhu Anālayo presents the Buddha's practical teaching of the path to nirvana in one comprehensive whole: the wheel of satipaṭṭhāna. *He writes for people who practise, and his own shines through like a beacon. This makes it a very exciting guide for practitioners – the truth of it leaps out at you. –* Kamalashila, author of *Buddhist Meditation: Tranquillity, Imagination and Insight*

ISBN 978 1 911407 10 2 | £14.99 / $19.95 / €17.95 | 256 pages